AF616019

Photo by Murrae Haynes

A scene from the New Mexico Repertory production of "Stumps." Set design by Jim

STUMPS

BY MARK MEDOFF

★

★

DRAMATISTS
PLAY SERVICE
INC.

STUMPS was produced by American Southwest Theatre Company (Kim McCallum, Artistic Director) in association with New Mexico State University in Las Cruces, New Mexico, on October 18, 1989. It was directed by Andrew Shea; the set and lighting designs were by Jim Billings; the costume design was by Barbara Agte; the sound design was by Joe Stanley; the original music was by Jan Scarbrough and performed by Scott Jarrett. The cast was as follows:

STEPHEN .... Edward Stone
JERRY .... Ross Marks
LIN .... Patti Yasutake
CAL .... Phil Reeves
EMILY .... Delia Copold

STUMPS was produced by New Mexico Repertory Theater (Andrew Shea, Artistic Director), in Albuquerque, New Mexico, in March, 1990. It was directed by Andrew Shea; the set and lighting designs were by Jim Billings; the costume design was by Catherine Zuber; the original music was by Jan Scarbrough and the stage manager was Maura J. Murphy. The cast was as follows:

STEPHEN .... Steven Schwartz-Hartley
JERRY .... Jim Holmes
LIN .... Patti Yasutake
CAL .... William Frankfather
EMILY .... Elizabeth Barondes

STUMPS was produced by Odyssey Theatre Ensemble (Ron Sossi, Artistic Director) in Los Angeles, California, in August, 1994. It was directed by Allan Miller; the set design was by Robert Steinberg; the costume design was by Joy Bodin and Ted Giammona; the lighting design was by Lawrence Oberman; the original music was by Jonathan Sacks and the production stage manager was David Pacifici. The cast was as follows:

STEPHEN .... Joseph Adams
JERRY .... Joe Maruzzo
LIN .... Patty Toy
CAL .... Gregg Henry
EMILY .... Alix Kormzay

STUMPS

ACT ONE

Scene 1

Two playing areas: Inside, the living room/kitchen area of a small trailer sitting in isolation on the river against the hill country outside Austin, Texas. Notable are a small but packed bookshelf and an electric piano. Outside, a "patio" area with a barbecue grill, two kids' toys and bikes (for ages 8 and 10), and some gardening utensils, potting soil, and pots. Two half gallon bottles of Septic Tank Dissolvent sit out.

Stephen Ryder, 31, works over a folder containing several sheets of paper; he uses the same hand that holds his pen to turn the pages, as only that one hand is real; the other, however, looks real. He wears a western suit.

Jerry Marcus, 30-35; he's in a wheelchair, paralyzed from the waist down; he wears expensive, preppy clothes. He's slicing zucchini on a small cutting board atop his lap.

Stephen's wife, Lin, 30-35, Vietnamese; she's dressed nicely but simply and works on a tray of cheese and crackers in the kitchen area, watching the Inauguration of Ronald Reagan on a small TV playing quietly on the counter separating the kitchen and living room.

It's January 20, 1981. As the lights and pre-show music fade, the sound of Ronald Reagan taking the oath of office from Chief Justice Warren Berger comes up and then under ...

STEPHEN. *Cheese?*

JERRY. Cheese, cheese, cheese, yeah, cheese!

STEPHEN. They think you're a rich Jewish kid from Chicago ...

JERRY. I'm not rich.

STEPHEN. ... and I'm this sophisticated financier from Austin. Believe me, they're not gonna think we're pretentious cuz a' cheese.

JERRY. Believe me, that's exactly what they are gonna think. That we're a coupla pretentious stumps. I say we should calmly, judiciously, and without ethnic or political considerations rethink our choice of appetizers.

STEPHEN. What is it, the trailer?

JERRY. I love the trailer.

STEPHEN. It's gotta be the trailer, cuz *it can't be the cheese.*

JERRY. It's definitely *not* the trailer and it *is* the cheese!

STEPHEN. You think Lin purposely picked out pretentious cheese?

JERRY. I think there's a good chance.

LIN. He's right, of course ...

JERRY. ... Immigrant chick trying to fit in, show off ...

LIN. ... I stood in the store and I thought: Let me see — Cheez Whiz? Velveeta ...

JERRY. ... What's wrong with Cheez Whiz?

LIN. ... Kraft slices ...

JERRY. ... See those squirt cans they have now — spritz it right onto your cracker — bang, you got a snack?

LIN. ... No, wait! What's this?

JERRY. The goddamn pretentious cheese section!

LIN. Yes! Bucheron and Montrachet will be wonderfully pretentious, so I'll get those.

JERRY. Okay, so maybe it isn't the cheese. Maybe I'm just a little edgy. Small psychotic episode in an otherwise balanced life. *(Jerry whacks at the zucchini.)*

STEPHEN. Ya know what I think?

JERRY. Nary a clue.

STEPHEN. I think you're still upset that he didn't mention anything about you in his last letter.

JERRY. Oh Jesus ...
STEPHEN. I think you're still eatin' yourself up over that.
JERRY. You know goddamn well the son of a bitch doesn't want to face the fact I'm the next goddamn Orson Welles.
LIN. You have to state your position calmly and articulately. Just don't allow yourself to become defensive and contentious.
JERRY. Lin, please.
LIN. Pretend I didn't speak.
JERRY. I'm serious, goddamn it! You're not my goddamn wife or my goddamn advisor.
STEPHEN. Say, Jer, you think Lin gave you any help in this deal or what?
JERRY. Isn't it pretty friggin' clear I'm grateful?
STEPHEN. If we keep our cool, Jer, we'll get everything we want.
JERRY. I'm cool, for Chrissake. I am. Okay, now I am. Okay, there, now I really am. *(For the first time, a moment of breathing space.)*
LIN. Jerry.
JERRY. Lin.
LIN. Please don't dice the zucchini.
JERRY. Now I'm dicing the zucchini. I hate that.
LIN. I asked you to make little strips — like this. *(She shows him some julienned carrots.)*
JERRY. You know what? I think — unconsciously of course — I was pretending to filet a Vietnamese schlong. *(Bringing the knife down hard and pronging a hunk.)* Whack! Gook Dong En Brochette. I'll try to properly slice the zucchini. *(The phone rings.)* That better not be them saying they're not coming or I swear to Christ, I'll ... *(Both men are concerned. Stare at the phone as Lin answers it.)*
LIN. Hello.... Hi, little one. What's the matter? Stephen, Linny's calling from the nurse's office. She has a headache. Mackie made her cry at recess. She wants to talk to Daddy. *(She pronounces Stephen's name "Stef'fan." Stephen is buried anxiously is his paperwork.)*
STEPHEN. I can't, you see me —
JERRY. I got it. *(He takes the phone.)* Miss Saralin Ryder, this

is your Uncle Nutty-buddy. Listen to me carefully: what I want you to do is, I want you to go find your sister and hit her in the stomach as hard as you can.

LIN. Thank you, Jerry, helpful as always.

JERRY. Yeah, well that pacifist crap you teach them —

LIN. Don't lecture me on what I teach my children. You are never available when people really need you.

JERRY. Screw you!

STEPHEN. Hey! *(He grabs the phone.)* Honey, honey, our guests are going to be here any minute.... No, no, sweetheart, Mommy and Uncle Jerry were just kidding. You tell your sister I said to be nice to you or else you guys aren't going to Beverly's for that slumber party tonight.... Your headache will go away, sweetheart, go back to class. Daddy loves you, don't fight! *(He sends several kisses into the phone and hangs it up.)* You two are worse than the kids.

LIN. Look, they did it.

STEPHEN. You hear what I — Who?

LIN. The Iranians. They released the hostages.

JERRY. Because our whacko friend the Ayatollah knows my man Ronaldo's at the helm now. Hold hostages on the Gipster, he'll blow 'em off the face of the friggin' earth!

LIN. You think that would be an effective way to bring them into the same world the rest of us want to live in, Jerry?

JERRY. Who wants 'em in the same world the rest of us wanna live in? Do to them what we shoulda done in Nam. Extirpate, subjugate, annihilate.

STEPHEN. Aw no, I knew I'd leave somethin' out. I left out the rental on the front-end loader.

LIN. They won't abandon you over a front-end loader. Don't write on that, Stephen. It's fine. *(It's very hard for Stephen to leave it.)*

JERRY. It's clean, it's pristine, it's white — leave it. *(Sound of car horn.)*

STEPHEN. Oh man ...

JERRY. Okay ...

STEPHEN. Okay, they're here.

JERRY. They're here.

STEPHEN. Okay, here they are.

JERRY. They're here.

STEPHEN. Jacket or no jacket? *(Stephen looks out an U. window.)*

JERRY. Ya look gorgeous.

STEPHEN. I feel like a game show host. *(Stephen's in the doorway now.)* Oh man, stumper, the future just showed up drivin' a Caddy Seville!

JERRY. What'd ya think he'd be drivin', a hundred-and-twelve-year-old Volkswagen like you?

STEPHEN. Holy crimanny! You're not gonna believe this.

JERRY. Try us.

STEPHEN. He's a priest!

LIN. A Catholic priest?

JERRY. How can he be a priest?

LIN. Maybe he has the wrong house.

STEPHEN. Uh-uh, she's with him. It's definitely her.

JERRY. I hope he is a priest. I hate all those religious bastards.

STEPHEN. No, you don't.

JERRY. So, do we kneel and kiss his ring?

STEPHEN. Don't start with him.

JERRY. I'm cool, stumper.

STEPHEN. Well, here goes everything. The house with the pool ...

JERRY. The limo with the wheelchair ramp ...

STEPHEN. Accepting the Oscar on national friggin' nationwide television!

JERRY. Brothers in grotesqueness, Stevie. *(Stephen and Jerry clasp hands. To Lin.)*

STEPHEN. Ya okay? *(She nods.)* We're doin' the right thing, right? I mean I don't mean it's wrong what we're doing, but I mean we're doing it the right way, right?

JERRY. The right thing is whatever it takes to get us from here to there. Orson Welles, Louis B. Mayer. Go! *(Stephen goes outside, to the patio. To Lin.)* You keep your mouth shut, don't interfere, don't interpret, don't referee. And, by the way, thanks for your help. It could've been more, but you did what you could.

Scene 2

Approaching are Calvin Rhodes, 35-50, and Emily "Rosenblum" (known professionally as Fawn Sierra), 18.

Emily is a young woman of startling physical beauty, one of those accidents of genetic coalescence. She wears horn-rim glasses, boots, jeans, and a sport coat with push-up sleeves — the urban "western" look of the early 80s. She carries a needlepoint bag. Her accent would suggest she grew up somewhere in the Deep South.

Cal indeed wears a black clerical suit, pastel dickey, and collar. He has a smile that's quite wonderful and a warmth that seems quite genuine. He carries a manila envelope. Stephen and Jerry both are drawn a number of times, if subtly, to this envelope; what's inside is important to them.

STEPHEN. Kinda put the driveway out there a ways so's folks'd really have to wanna pay us a visit to get on in here.
CAL. As it says in Isaiah, "This is the way, walk ye in it." Do I have the privilege at last of addressing Mr. Steve Ryder?
STEPHEN. Well, I don't know about the privilege, but yessir, it's me for sure.
CAL. Greetings, my friend, from our shared dreams. *(Stephen offers his hand. Cal ignores the hand and takes Stephen into his arms, gives him a big hug.)*
STEPHEN. Well, thank you very much, Mr. Rhodes. Or Father Rhodes, I guess it is. Thanks just a whole heckuva lot, Father.
CAL. Not Father, Steve. I'm afraid celibacy was never an option for me. Reverend Rhodes, Pastor Rhodes, or just Cal.

As my momma used to say, "Call me anything ya like, just don't call me late for supper."

STEPHEN. Yessir. And this here must be Miss Sierra.

CAL. Indeed it is.

STEPHEN. I can't tell ya how really swell it is to have you standin' right here, your very own self on my patio.

EMILY. It's awful nice to be here, Mr. Ryder.

STEPHEN. This your first trip to these parts?

EMILY. Yessir. Thought there'd be, like, cows everywhere.

STEPHEN. Oh, there's cows; people just don't keep 'em so much around the house anymore, if ya know what I mean. My neighbor over there a ways, though, he's got chickens.

EMILY. Really! We had chickens down home. Does he ever bring yawl over fresh eggs in the mornin'?

STEPHEN. Nope, sure doesn't.

EMILY. Aw, shoot, he should; we had us a neighbor once did that.

STEPHEN. Mine there, he pretty much considers me the scum a' the earth. Well, come right on in, Jerry's prob'ly bout ready to pop a gut, waitin'. *(They go inside.)* Jerry, right here's Miss Fawn Sierra and just right here's the Rev. Calvin Rhodes. Miss Sierra, Pastor, may I present my partner here, Jerry Marcus, the writer.

CAL. A pleasure, Mr. Marcus.

JERRY. Jerry's just fine, Cal. Miss Sierra, how're you?

EMILY. Just fine, thank you.

STEPHEN. And this here over here is my wife, Lin. Pastor Rhodes and Miss Fawn Sierra, Lin.

CAL. *Buenos dias, Señora, y muchas gracias por invitarnos a su casa.*

LIN. I'm sorry, I don't speak Spanish.

CAL. I'm terribly sorry, I thought you were Latina.

LIN. Vietnamese.

CAL. I'm terribly sorry.

LIN. It's quite all right.

CAL. Haven't even dispensed with the amenities, and I've insulted my hostess.

STEPHEN. Na, now, Pastor, you didn't insult anybody.

CAL. I'm terribly sorry, Mrs. Ryder.
LIN. Really, it's all right.
CAL. May I ask if anyone tried to contact me here by telephone?
LIN. No.
CAL. Gentleman named Carlos — who actually is Latino.
LIN. No.
CAL. Well, sugar! Thought I heard the phone ring as we were gettin' outta the car.
LIN. It was for us.
CAL. Certainly no reason you shouldn't receive phone calls at your own home. *(Cal smiles his luminous smile.)* May I ask what you're watching so intently there on TV?
LIN. The inauguration.
CAL. Of course.
LIN. And they just released the hostages.
CAL. Ah yes.... And now, exactly which hostages are those?
LIN. In Iran. *(A beat. We're not sure if he knows what she's talking about.)*
CAL. Well, that's wonderful news, isn't it? Great news indeed.
JERRY. Say, Cal, I don't mean to start right out here on a note of doubt ...
CAL. Start on any note you like, Jerry,
JERRY. ... but you're not really a reverend, are ya — I mean, seriously?
CAL. Oh, indeed I am. A bit distant from the main flock at this point, but a man of the cloth nevertheless. Does that trouble you or otherwise compromise our working together?
STEPHEN. No, course not. Jerry just meant it kinda startled us.
CAL. You may recall, my friends, that Jesus himself did not limit himself to trafficking solely with the chaste and irreproachable.
EMILY. This sure is an awful sweet set-up yawl got here, Mrs. Ryder — gosh.
LIN. Thank you
EMILY. How much land yawl got?

LIN. We have five acres.

EMILY. Oh, wow. And it just smells like people live here.

STEPHEN. If yawl look out there right here, you can see it out there, we're buildin' us a little house right to the west there. *(They have a look, Cal hovering behind Emily and Stephen.)*

EMILY. Oh, look, Calvin!

CAL. Oh, yes.

STEPHEN. That there's the foundation. Lin designed it and I'm doing all the subcontracting. 'Bout ready to frame 'er up.

EMILY. And the river just right there and all those trees! Oh yeah!

JERRY. Yeah, so, okay, Cal, Steve, whudduya say, could we ... *(Jerry indicates sitting and getting on with it.)*

CAL. I'd be happy to get down to business, Jerry ... just as soon as Emily's through rhapsodizing about domiciles and landscape.

EMILY. I'm through.

CAL. Don't let us rush you.

EMILY. You didn't.

STEPHEN. Pastor Cal, why don't you sit right here on the sofa here.

CAL. If you don't mind, I'll stand.

STEPHEN. Oh sure, hey, you bet.

CAL. Emily, would you like to sit down? *(Emily looks at Cal, seeming to await the decision from him.)* Simple decision, Emily: sit or stand?

EMILY. Can I needlepoint?

CAL. Would anyone object if Emily were to needlepoint?

STEPHEN. Course not. *(Emily sits, takes out her needlepoint. Her stroke is sharp and suggests the need to sublimate a lot of energy.)*

JERRY. You call her Emily...?

CAL. Ah. Given name: Emily Laurel Rosenblum. Her father's an Orthodox rabbi; in deference to him and the family's social standing in Birmingham, we concocted a *nom du cinema*. *(Emily no more than flicks her eyes at Cal.)*

JERRY. Would you prefer we Call you Emily or Fawn?

EMILY. What happened to you?

CAL. Emily, what a question to ask someone you just met.
EMILY. I'm sorry, Calvin, but it's a little hard to pretend not to notice.
JERRY. Don't worry about it. I'd just as soon get it outta the way.
CAL. Good for you, Jerry.
JERRY. Excuse me, Cal, please don't say, "Good for me." It's no great accomplishment to talk about what happened. Got a little text all planned, push a button, comes right out. I stepped on a land mine, Emily. Take my foot off, it blows. Keep my foot on it, it doesn't.
CAL. Vietnam, Jerry?
JERRY. No land mines over here, Cal.
CAL. Though I shouldn't think it'll be long now.
EMILY. How come somebody didn't defuse it?
JERRY. Nobody spotted me from the air. They thought the whole squad was dead.
EMILY. How long did you stand there with your foot on it?
JERRY. Two and a half days.
EMILY. You stood there for two and a half days?
JERRY. Given the alternatives, didn't seem all that long.
CAL. What made you finally give up, Jerry?
JERRY. I didn't give up, Cal.
CAL. I'm sure that was an ill-chosen phrase.
JERRY. I don't give up.
CAL. An admirable approach to life — one to which I wish more people subscribed.
EMILY. You just couldn't stand up forever.
JERRY. Sniper finally blew my knees out till I went down. Six rounds. Four in this one, two in this one. The mine was a dud. Didn't go off. Sniper shot me in the spine for good measure.
EMILY. Oh no.
STEPHEN. They nail you with a tour over there, Pastor Cal?
CAL. No, no they didn't. Trick knee, of all things. Old football injury. And to be quite truthful, I was a member of the loyal opposition, so to speak — running an underground rail-

way for draft resistors into Canada.

JERRY. Well, gee, that just warms my heart, Cal.

CAL. Each of us must abide his conscience. Well, we're certainly excited to see your facility tonight, Steve.

STEPHEN. Oh, yessir. And you're gonna be right surprised, I think, at the type of folks that come to my theatre. Twenty-eight percent of our clientele's ladies, which I'm sure you realize is way above average for an X-rated movie house.

EMILY. From what you described in your letters, it really sounds neat.

STEPHEN. Yes, ma'am, I think it is. I kinda fixed the place up real nice, started servin' food and beverages like they do in your cinema art houses that show all your top-rated foreign films and like that, and I only book in films where the man and the woman are treated kinda pretty equal; no perverse stuff, no violence. *(Stephen's glance at Lin might indicate to us that she had a hand in the creation of this agenda.)*

CAL. I've long felt that many women would benefit from availing themselves of our product; always find their caterwauling about "dirty old men" and "denigration of women" rather deceitful; I think you may have hit upon the secret, however: respect for women. Indeed. Couldn't help noticing some of your books here, Steve. Not gonna report ya, ya understand — but Camus, Sartre, Genet?

STEPHEN. Oh, well I was takin' a course over to the university — that's what the teacher — the professor — that's what he assigned us. That's where Jerry and me met — in that class. Got to talkin' bout The Nam and how nobody wasn't hardly writin' nothin' or makin' any movies 'bout our experience over there, next thing ya know he shows me some of his secret writin' and I'm confessin' some a' my own secret aspirations and — *(Cal plays several chords on the piano.)*

CAL. And who, may I ask, plays the piano?

STEPHEN. Both our girls play. Lin's teachin 'em herself.

CAL. You design houses, you teach piano ...

STEPHEN. She's written a real dandy love theme we're tryin to convince her to let us use in the film.

CAL. "Convince"? Not sure you want to lend your music to

this enterprise, Mrs. Ryder?

LIN. I am trying to be supportive.

CAL. I'd like very much to hear your music. Which, I believe in musical terminology is called a segue, and I suppose properly brings us to this. *(He indicates the manila envelope.)*

JERRY. Kill the TV, Lin. Please. If ya wouldn't mind. *(A beat. Lin turns the TV off.)*

STEPHEN. So, what'd you think of Jerry's script, Pastor Cal?

CAL. I think it's all that you said it would be. And I think it actually can be all you dream it might be.

STEPHEN. Ya hear that, Jer?

JERRY. I'm sittin' right here, stumper.

CAL. Now, according to your correspondence, Steve, when you saw *No End In Sight,* you both felt Emily was the right actress to play Catherine.

JERRY. Absolutely.

STEPHEN. The only actress to play Catherine.

CAL. Well, that's even more flattering. Isn't it, Emily?

EMILY. It's amazing, you guys. I dream about making a movie where I'd have the chance to —

CAL. When you first wrote, I said to Emily: Read this young man Ryder's letters. Am I crazy or does he have the passion of a crusader? And to be truthful with you, what your epistles made us realize, Steve, is that we have an obligation — a moral obligation, in point of fact — not to make anything remotely like a standard explicit motion picture ever again.

EMILY. Right after *No End In Sight* came out and I was a little wee bit famous — or infamous, I guess to some folks — Calvin and me were tryin' to figure out what's the best way to make the jump to legitimate film and then your first letter came, Mr. Ryder, and Calvin says read this, and I do: "Dear Miss Sierra, We haven't ever met in person, in the light of day, but I'm wondering if I'm in a dream you dream. Listen here and tell me if you see me in there." *(Lin is hearing these words for the first time.)* Well, maybe it wasn't exactly poetry, but it sure wasn't the usual gobbledygook I get.

STEPHEN. Flowed out as natural as breathin'. Only worked

on those first sentences a coupla weeks.
EMILY. Mrs. Ryder, I bet he wrote you beautiful letters when you were first goin' together.
LIN. No.... But he has a very poetic spirit — you're right.
JERRY. Ya know, gang, just on the off-chance we're *not* gonna film Steve's letters, I'm wondering if we're ever gonna get around to discussing my frigging script, which is ultimately the son of a bitching means to achieving everyone's fabulous mother-humping goals.
CAL. Just what is your problem, son?
JERRY. Gee, do I have the problem?
STEPHEN. He's just a little ticked off, Pastor Cal that —
JERRY. Bag it, Steve.
STEPHEN. No! He was upset that ya had the script for two weeks and then when ya said you'd come on down, ya never said a word about the script or his other involvement in the project.
CAL. I see.
JERRY. And then ya walk in here and you're talking about Steve's letters ...
CAL. Hey you, hey you!
JERRY. ... like they're goddamn works of art!
CAL. Who brought you here, you?
JERRY. What?
CAL. Steve!
JERRY. Steve *what?*
CAL. "Steve *what?*" Steve's vision brought you to this project! Steve's commitment brought me *and* Emily to your script. And it is your frigging script that's gonna make this son of a bitching venture utterly singular. But not now, not as it is! The fact is, your script isn't as good yet as this young man's passion for it ... or mine and Emily's for what it can be. This young man sold us a *possibility*. And if you're going to continure this juvenile, self-serving crap, I'm going the hell home and taking her with me and that's gonna be the son of a bitching end of this!... Now, may I proceed? *(A beat.)*
STEPHEN. Please, go on, Pastor Cal.
CAL. And can I be blunt or do I have to waste a lot of

time tiptoeing around your feelings? Whudduya say, can you handle some honest criticism?

JERRY. Only one way to find out.

CAL. Then let's do, let's find out. Why don't we begin in the beginning, with the title:

EMILY. *Catherine Liberty.*

CAL. *Catherine Liberty.* Nice title. I like the implications of the Delacroix print Josh has on his wall. Very telling, but —

EMILY. "Liberty Leading the People."

CAL. Why don't you go on, Emily?

EMILY. Oh no, Calvin.

CAL. — But I raise the question whether we want to spend four static, uneventful pages at the moment Catherine and Josh first meet validating the title of the film by talking about this painting of a beefy, unattractive female with her breasts exposed leading a group of hopeless miscreants into battle.

JERRY. Do I respond or should I keep my mouth shut?

CAL. Oh, for goodness sake, Jerry, come on; of course, respond; at least in theory, we're working together on this. Now, please.

JERRY. Okay. First of all, I don't see those four pages as static and uneventful; she's just had the crap beat out of her by her boyfriend, so it's not like we haven't started the movie with a little excitement; second, they're preparing dinner and engaging in an amusing and flirtatious argument about ingredients *while* they discuss the painting.

CAL. "Amusing and flirtatious" — all right, maybe I have to see it to find it amusing and —

LIN. It's also implied, I think, Jerry, by the painting itself, that at some level, all wars, whether physical or verbal, are fought for a woman's breasts. *(Everyone looks at Lin.)*

JERRY. Right.

CAL. Yes, yes, of course, Josh's realization that he became paralyzed, lost his freedom, because he hoped to come home a hero, a Man — with a capital "M" —

LIN. I think his realization is more complex than that, Mr. Rhodes. It has to do with capital "M" Motherhood ...

CAL. Motherhood.

LIN. ... and the love-hate relationship men have with women and why the Khmer Rouge in Cambodia slaughter girl babies but not boy babies and —

CAL. Pardon me, Mrs. Ryder — the Khmer Rouge are in this? Are you doing a dissertation on this script or something? Are you Jerry's dramaturge?

JERRY. No, she's not.

LIN. We talked a lot about making Catherine a three-dimensional character.

JERRY. You mind?

LIN. Sorry.

CAL. Look, there's no doubt whatsoever that you've got some beautifully expressed views of the human condition in this script, but you know what I'm afraid of? I'm afraid our audience is going to find our main characters pretentious and — by extension — the main characters' *creator* — and consultant — even more pretentious. Now what's potentially stunning about this script is the sheer fury of the relationship. It makes Brando and Schneider in *Last Tango* look ... well, like Ozzie and Harriet. *(Glancing at his watch.)* Excuse me, could I get a glass of something liquid to drink?

STEPHEN. Course. Lin, could you ... *(Cal takes a plastic bottle of medication out of his jacket pocket, pops the top, shakes out two capsules.)* We got beer, coffee, iced tea. Or we got us a nice little bottle a' wine to go with this here cheese here. I thought ya might like somethin' to snack on. Ya like cheese, Miss Sierra — Emily?

EMILY. Oh no, thank you, Mr. Ryder, I don't eat dairy products.

STEPHEN. Oh shoot, ya don't? Aw, great. Jeez, Lin, what else we —

EMILY. No, really, I —

STEPHEN. It's no problem, we got us a whole fridge there fulla ... Lin, whuddo we —

LIN. I have some ham slices and some baloney. Would you like a sandwich or —

JERRY. Ham, Lin? Baloney? Coming from an Orthodox Jewish Birmingham family?

CAL. Please don't concern yourself, Mrs. Ryder. We had a late breakfast at our hotel. "The Texas Special," Steve. Two pigs in a blanket, sunnyside up egg, a dollop of those mashed up beans, and a stack a tortillas we could sleep under on a cold night. I'll have wine, Mrs. Ryder, she'll have water.

EMILY. I didn't have "The Texas Special," Calvin. I had sliced tomatoes and half a grapefruit.

CAL. Oh, this is very nice cheese, Mrs. Ryder. Bucheron and — Don't tell me.... Montrachet?

LIN. Yes.

CAL. *C'est magnifique!*

LIN. *Rien.*

CAL. Jerry? *(Jerry declines. Cal holds the tray toward Stephen.)* Steve? *Stephen reaches for the tray with both hands — the real one and the prosthetic one ... seeming to startle Cal.)* Whoa — oh my! *(He jars everyone in the room.)* I'm sorry, didn't mean to startle everyone. It wasn't until just this moment that I realized Steve has only one hand. Forgive me — you'd think I'd never seen an artificial limb before. My land, you hide that well. May I be as blunt as Emily and ask how you lost it? *(Stephen pours the wine.)*

STEPHEN. Oh, you know, decided to leave somethin' over in The Nam – little remembrance of my havin' gone on over to help those folks demolish their country.

CAL. *(In sympathy and anger.)* Mmph! Mmph mmph mmph mmph mmph — uh-uh-uh, don't bite your fingernails, Emily.

LIN. Excuse me, Mr. Rhodes ...

CAL. Yes?

LIN. If she doesn't eat ham — Emily — wouldn't it seem logical she wouldn't eat sausage?

CAL. I'm sorry, did I just miss something? *(Stephen hands Cal his wine; Cal swallows a capsule.)*

LIN. You said she ate "The Texas Special."

CAL. Yes.

LIN. She said she didn't.

CAL. Right.

LIN. If she doesn't eat ham, it seems logical to me she wouldn't have eaten sausage.

CAL. Very observant, Mrs. Ryder. Very keen observation. But as I recall — Emily, correct me if I'm wrong here — we both ordered "The Texas Special" and I ate the sausage off of both plates. Am I right on that, Emily, or do I have that cock-eyed?

EMILY. *(Short beat.)* No, you're right, Calvin.

CAL. I believe it was yesterday you had sliced tomatoes and half a grapefruit.

EMILY. That's right.

CAL. Have I offended you too in some way, Mrs. Ryder?

STEPHEN. No, hey, course not.

JERRY. Just ignore her. She's not what you call a big fan of the project.

CAL. I'm a little confused about who doesn't care for whom here. Now, am I to assume you're on your side against me, Jerry, but my side against Mrs. Ryder? Yet, Mrs. Ryder seems to have a certain interest in the character of Catherine, if not the script as a —

LIN. I was a "fan of the project" when it was a story Jerry was writing which he and Stephen hoped to turn into a real movie.

CAL. I see, yes. "Real movie." I understand, Mrs. Ryder, that it's not easy to accept the potential healing power of this enterprise; I regret that the marriage of the erotic and art to God offends you.

LIN. I have no illusions about God or the people who represent themselves as representing Him. I simply don't want, at the most basic level, to see my husband and this very good writer making pornography because they imagine it is the only way to get from here to where they want to go.

CAL. Divorce him.

LIN. What?

CAL. Your husband has been involved in pornography for some time, has he not? Leave him. Dump the scum.

LIN. I think there is a difference between showing the type of explicit movies he shows and making this.

CAL. Well, some time when I have no other agenda, Mrs. Ryder, I would love to listen to you hold forth on that distinction. I believe in what I do, Mrs. Ryder, I believe in this project, and you must understand that your disapproval will not sway me — nor clearly, these men — from our chosen course a single millimeter.

EMILY. You might like to know, Mrs. Ryder, that every little penny of profit from *No End In Sight* goes to Calvin's foundation for Runaway Children. Every single little penny.

LIN. Perhaps I'm being unfair, but I find that very difficult to believe.

CAL. Jerry's hostility I can accept as part of the package, Steve, but if I'm going to have to contend with your wife's as well, let me suggest we go back to our hotel and continue our discussion there.

JERRY. What the hell for? This is Steve's house too. We're here, we've already wasted half an hour talking about nothing. Let's just get on with it!

STEPHEN. I think we should stay on here. But I think we oughta all of us endeavor not to be wastin' energy with a lotta peacockin', now I really do. And that goes for everyone. Now why don't we just move on outside — git some air and settle down to gittin' some work done.

CAL. I think that's an excellent idea.

JERRY. Yeah, okay, I agree, but let's do it, let's go. *Stephen opens the door, sets up the ramp for Jerry as ... Emily gets up, purse in hand.)*

EMILY. Could I use your rest room?

LIN. Of course. First door on the left.

CAL. Why, sweetheart?

EMILY. I just need to go potty.

CAL. Are you feeling all right?

EMILY. Yes. It's just that, you know, all that coffee I drank at —

CAL. Let's leave your purse.

EMILY. But I need to —

CAL. Why don't you let me hold your purse, sweetheart.

EMILY. *(Leaning close.)* Calvin, I really need to go potty. But I need my purse. I want to freshen up my —

CAL. Your make-up looks fine, sweetheart. You look beautiful.

EMILY. Never mind.

CAL. No potty? *(Emily shakes her head.)* You're sure? *(Emily nods.)* Take your medicine. *(Cal holds out a capsule to her. She swallows it; senses Lin looking at her.)*

EMILY. My medicine. *(Lin nods.)*

CAL. You don't have to explain yourself to anyone, sweetheart.

EMILY. I was just —

CAL. Don't. *(Emily goes past Cal and down the ramp to the patio. A beat between Cal and Lin.)* Would it be fair to assume that you and Jerry had a sexual entanglement at some point your husband isn't aware of?

LIN. What?

CAL. I won't say anything. Believe me, I understand the labyrinth of the human heart. *(Before Lin can respond, Cal is out the door and approaching Stephen, Jerry, and Emily.)* My my, air that doesn't smell of human foible. Mmph. Any fish in that river, Steve?

STEPHEN. You better believe it.

CAL. Trout?

STEPHEN. No sir, 'fraid not. But plenty a' bass, carp, crappee. So, back to this. *(He holds up the script.)*

CAL. I suppose before I try again to discuss the script with Jerry, we should address what I suspect will be our most difficult subject.

STEPHEN. Our plan to have Jerry direct the film and also play Josh. We know it's a little unusual for the first time out —

JERRY. If Charlie Chaplin and Woody Allen can do it, why can't I?

CAL. Forgive me, Jerry, but I really don't think you can compare yourself to Charlie Chaplin and Woody Allen just yet.

JERRY. They had to write, direct, and star in their first films at some point, didn't they?

CAL. Kids, lemme just state my position and be done with it: We have to get rid of the paralysis altogether. And we have to employ —

JERRY. — Employ a physically able-bodied actor and load Josh up with some "psychic wound," delayed stress, maybe, so we don't make our audience worry about whether, when his clothes are removed, Josh's legs are going to be emaciated or, heaven forbid, he's catheterized or had a colostomy and he's wearing a bag connected to his intestines. Have I got that about right, Cal?

CAL. Just about.

EMILY. Calvin thinks Josh should be played by the funny Black guy on *Saturday Night Live.*

CAL. Do you mind if I speak for myself, Emily?

EMILY. No, Calvin.

CAL. No matter how diversified our audience may become, the overwhelming majority of them will be Caucasian ladies and gentlemen who secretly yearn to either *be* or be taken *by* a large Black man with a Louisville Slugger size penis.

JERRY. You gotta be kidding.

CAL. Indeed I'm not. As for the directing matter my preference would be to bring in —

JERRY. — Bring in an experienced director, I go to school on him, and then the next script you'll very seriously consider me as the director.

CAL. No need for me to speak at all, is there? You and Emily can just speak for me.

JERRY. I couldn't agree to any of that. Couldn't, can't, won't. None of it.

EMILY. Calvin just wants what's best for everyone, Jerry. Really. Don't you, Calvin?

CAL. Is that a question for me, Emily?

JERRY. So, is that it? Ya got anything else?

CAL. Yes. The matter of Catherine's character. If the critics and the public are to view this film not as a porno film but, as Steve said in his first letter, the next step beyond *Last Tango In Paris,* I seriously question whether Catherine should be an art history major; my feeling is she has to have considerably less dialogue and the dialogue she does have must be considerably less educated — if you really believe Emily is the right actress for the role. You noticed, needless to say, that Emily has no lines in *No End In Sight.*

EMILY. But it was moronic, Calvin. I was playing a girl who had her vocal chords cut out by the Mafia.

CAL. And you may even have thought that was a brilliant stroke of plotting to engage audience sympathy for our heroine ...

JERRY. Nope, figured it was just plain bad writing.

CAL. Well, sad to say, it was a purely pragmatic decision, based on the fact that Emily is more adept at physicalizing her emotions than she is at vocalizing them.

EMILY. I don't think I was given what you'd call a real fair chance to show what I could —

CAL. Emily — goodness! Must we always deal in subterfuge?

EMILY. I don't know what that means, but you are exaggerating and so I'm speaking up in my own —

CAL. You're very talkative today, Emily. For whom are you showing off?

JERRY. Course I'm just an amateur, but what I saw you do in *No End In Sight* when you were relating to people in a normal way, I thought displayed a helluva lotta promise.

EMILY. Thank you, Jerry. There — see, Calvin —

CAL. You're very angry at me, Jerry ...

JERRY. I'm not angry at you.

CAL. ... and despite the fact that I'd like to take a crowbar to your skull right now, I'm not going to let this discussion devolve again into unpleasantness.

JERRY. Have no fear of a devolving conversation, Cal, 'cause I'm not angry at you.

CAL. You asked me for my suggestions and I've given them to you.

JERRY. Well, I didn't exactly ask for 'em.

CAL. Well, you damn well should have! I'm the one with the distributor and the crew and the insurance company with the completion bond, so you should very goddamn well beg me to make suggestions to you!

STEPHEN. I hate to say it, reverend, but the conversation's kinda taken a pretty ferocious devolving turn here —

CAL. But, hey, listen, there are other producers, there are other young women with followings.

JERRY. There may be other producers — I don't figure film producers are an endangered species, — but I want Emily.

CAL. Let me put it another way: There's no way in hell you get Emily without me!

JERRY. Yeah, well there's no way in hell I'm gutting the language or the substance outta my script, and if I don't direct and play the role, we got no deal!

STEPHEN. *Are you guys gonna cut this stuff out or what!* Now I've about had it, fellas, I'm not kiddin' ya! This ain't worth it if I'm gonna end up with an ulcer the first doggone day! I worked real goddarn hard to get us four all together here.

CAL. Well, I can't seem to do anything to please Jerry, Steve. If you can arbitrate between us, then please do.

STEPHEN. Fine, my pleasure. Binding arbitration though. What I say —

CAL. What do you want, Jerry, huh?

STEPHEN. Thank you, Cal, I'll stand over here, just tell me when to start arbitrating —

CAL. What, Jerry? You want me simply to give you Carlos' check for 200,000 and deposit it and Emily here with you and let you go out and buy some Super-8 and pretend you're Bertolucci?

JERRY. If you had all these problems, why'd you come all the way down here from New York?

CAL. I came all the way down here because you can write, my friend. Content yourself with being the creator of this — potentially — important erotic film in praise of women, this film that explores not just their storied sexuality, their legendary availability as victims, but their ability to resurrect the emotionally dead.

JERRY. Why do I feel like you're blowin' smoke up my ass?

CAL. Forgive me if I slighted you by not responding in my letter to Steve about your script and the acting and directing matters, but I chose to do so in person; if I'm not doing it well now that I'm here, I *am* doing it as well as I *can.* Now,

I think you must ask yourself if you're receiving what I'm saying as well as *you* can.
JERRY. All right, you're right, I hear you, I'm not always consistent in my behavior, and maybe I have a little problem with men who have the gift of tongues and stand on two fully functioning legs, but just let me have my say, okay?
CAL. Absolutely.
JERRY. I've got a degree in theatre. I'm finishing an MFA in film. While I'm not a totally physically, able-bodied actor, and my penis is white, or beige really, and perhaps a few inches short of Louisville slugger dimension, I am sexually capable and I am a damn good actor. Which seem to me to be the two main prerequisites for the character. And I know I can direct this film effectively. *(A beat. Jerry indicates he's said what he wants to say.)*
CAL. Thank you. I understand your position. Let me give the various matters some further thought, and let me ask Carlos to do the same. Does that seem fair? Steve, is there some place I can make a private call — collect, of course?
STEPHEN. Jer, is that fair, Cal's askin' ya?
CAL. Steve.
STEPHEN. I'm sorry, Cal, what?
CAL. Phone, phone, I gotta make a call.
STEPHEN. Oh sure — go right on inside and back there to the back bedroom.
CAL. Can I ask you to do me an enormous favor and trot out to the car and get that little leather cigar case off the front seat?
STEPHEN. Sure, be glad to. *(Stephen goes off.)*
CAL. Little Bub, can I trust you to conduct yourself discreetly while I'm gone? *(Emily nods. Cal heads up the ramp.)*
JERRY. Does that mean we're forbidden to speak?
EMILY. Don't get him any more mad at you, please. I meet so many guys with some kinda irresistible need to self-destruct — it makes me so damn mad.
JERRY. Pretty big notion there, Emily, for someone who can't vocalize. *(Emily moves with her needlepoint away from Jerry. Cal stares at Lin a moment from behind, through the screen door of*

the trailer. Sensing someone, she turns. Cal enters.)

CAL. Your husband said I could use the phone. *(Lin indicates the phone on the counter.)* The one in the bedroom. You can come with me if you'd like to make sure I don't touch or look at anything I shouldn't. *(His smile.)*

LIN. If Stephen says it's all right ...

CAL. The way you look at me with those luminous eyes is quite extraordinary, as if you might see me in a light the others can't. Perhaps you'll be kind enough to share those insights with me at some point.

LIN. I have never cheated on my husband.

CAL. And is that the extent of what you want to say to me? *(A beat. She smiles.)* Something amusing?

LIN. Yes. Hostages are coming home after more than a year in captivity, a new President is carrying the hopes of the Free World, and we're doing this. Don't you find that somewhat amusing? *(She stares at him, he at her.)*

CAL. I think I do, yes. Yes, I believe I see the humor there. *(He lifts a hand toward her face. She pulls back.)* Some sort of vegetation protruding from the end of your nose. May I? *(He reaches again, she pulls back, swipes at her nose. She goes to the plate of cheese, takes it quickly outside. Cal goes down the hall.)*

Scene 3

Stephen returns with Cal's cigar case. Lin lingers a moment on the rampway outside the door of the trailer.

STEPHEN. In case you haven't noticed, the man's very damn intelligent; some a' the criticisms he had about the script there —

JERRY. Excuse me, Stephen, but why don't ya see if you can get your nose all the way up his ass and go for *The Guinness Book of Records.*

STEPHEN. I'm just protecting what I believe in. Now, are we gonna prove we're more than a coupla stumps or are you gonna screw this up cuz he's not kissin' your handicapped ass? *(Lin comes down the ramp, puts the cheese on the picnic table.)*

JERRY. Emily. You read the script. *(When she doesn't respond.)* He can't hear us. You read the script and you like it a lot, don't you?... You do, I know you do. You think you can act this role, don't you? *(A beat. She nods once.)* You know and he knows this could change your life. Right? *(A beat.)* Right? *(Emily nods. Lin collects a sneaker and several of the children's toys and stuffed animals that are sitting around the patio area.)* Would you be willing to read a scene from the script with me? *(She looks after Cal.)* We'll ask him first. If he says it's okay, are you willing to read a scene with me — we'll both show him what we can do?

EMILY. Will you tell me the truth if ya think I *can't* do it?

JERRY. I promise. *(Inside, Cal comes out of the bedroom. He begins to doctor the sauce simmering on the stove.)*

EMILY. I'm sorry, Mrs. Ryder, I know it must not be real great havin' us here and I'm sorry we have to be, but this is like real kinda important to me too, ya know.

LIN. It's complicated for all of us, Emily.

EMILY. Yes, ma'am, thank you.

LIN. Stephen, listen to me, if you can ...

CAL. *(Calling.) Smells mighty good in here!*

EMILY. Oh no. Okay, don't anybody say I was talkin' to you, okay?

CAL. *(Calling.) Smells ... (Cal lets a gob of spit ooze out of his mouth and into the simmering sauce.) ... absolutely divine! (He gives the sauce a stir ... and heads for the door.)*

LIN. Take a walk with me.

STEPHEN. Now? I can't.

LIN. There's something wrong here.

STEPHEN. I don't have time for this.

LIN. I'm going for a walk.

STEPHEN. What about the preparations for afterward tonight?

CAL. *(Coming down the ramp.)* What's going on afterward tonight?

STEPHEN. Lin'd like to cook yawl up one of her special

deals — little late-night supper, if that's all right?

CAL. That sounds positively sensational, doesn't it, Em? *(Lin goes back inside, gets a lightweight Dallas Cowboys zipper jacket.)*

EMILY. *(Calling after Lin.)* Yeah, but please don't do it if you're only doin' it 'cause ya think ya gotta. I mean, Calvin'd be happy to take everyone to the hotel for dinner, wouldn't ya, Calvin?

CAL. Sure, hotel slop sounds great.

STEPHEN. We're gonna do it here. We been plannin' it.

EMILY. Well, if you're sure.

STEPHEN. I'm sure.

CAL. May we go on now with business, Emily?

EMILY. I'm sorry, Calvin, I was just tryin' to help.

CAL. Thank you sweetheart, but don't. All right, Jerry, I conferred with Carlos; he'll review the matter. However, I think it only fair I inform you Emily's got a confirmed offer that's going to be hard to turn down if this arrangement continues to prove problematical.

JERRY. I'd like Emily to read a scene from the script with me. I'd really like the opportunity to show you what —

CAL. I think that's an excellent idea. Good. Fine. *(Lin comes back out the door, starts off-stage to the side opposite the patio.)*

STEPHEN. Lin, don't do this! I thought you'd come to terms with what we wanna do with this film.

LIN. I thought I had. But it was less obscene when it was just the two of you sitting in our living room with your masturbatory fantasies.

STEPHEN. It's not obscene, damn you!

LIN. I'm sorry — I know it's more than that. But this is a mistake.

CAL. You needn't be jealous of Emily, Mrs. Ryder.

LIN. Jealous of Emily?

CAL. You're her equal in every way, I'm sure. Wouldn't you say, Steve?

STEPHEN. 'Scuse me here a second, Cal —

LIN. You mean this is only a problem I have, Mr. Rhodes? You mean I only question this enterprise because I feel threatened? But all right, yes, it's embarrassing for me to see the way my husband looks at her, but not just for me, for him too.

STEPHEN. Listen, could we have this conversation in private, ya think?

LIN. Have you forgotten how long when you were in the hospital we dreamed of a piece of land by a river where my children and I could live in peace with you, a family? Until this movie came into our life, we were both building that dream and that house block by block.

STEPHEN. Don'cha think I know what debts I owe, Lin, and who I owe 'em to.

LIN. *(A beat; to the others.)* I'm sorry ... *(And to Stephen.)* ... I swore I wasn't going to make this difficult. I love you and you're my friend — or you were. *(She goes off.)*

CAL. Steve, when I get home, I'd like to send your wife some literature.... Well, while these two young troupers work on their scene, why don't you and I go down to the river and throw a line in the water?

STEPHEN. Sure, hey, whatever you want. I put the whole day aside. Lemme grab the rods and the tackle box. *(Stephen gets the tackle box and two rods out of the storage box on the patio.)*

CAL. Did you know, kids, that we came from fish? It's true. We're just a little transmutational fluke. If you were to throw the evolutionary dice again, chances are we wouldn't show up at all.

STEPHEN. And that'd be a real shame. *(Indicating the two jugs of dissolvent.)* If you'll grab those two jugs there, Pastor Cal — I need to dump that stuff on the way. *(Cal grabs the jugs.)*

CAL. This is a mean looking libation.

STEPHEN. Yeah, well everybody's on septic tanks out here. Gotta feed 'em every six weeks or they tend to return what ya send 'em right back up to your house.

CAL. Looks like you could dissolve Emily's mother's matzo balls in this. But I guess when you're dealing with excrement, ya can't fool around. *(He smiles his smile and turns to Emily.)* May I have a private word with you, Little Bub? *(They step*

aside.) You want me to treat you like a grown-up girl?
EMILY. Yes.
CAL. Want me to let you help make decisions and formulate policy?
EMILY. Yes.
CAL. Then let me hold your purse and keep your goddamn mouth shut. *(Cal takes her purse and brings her gently, sweetly to him. A love chant.)* Is-a-baby, is-a-baby, is-a-sweetie-wittle-baby. Fishie kiss, fishie kiss, give a boy a fishie kiss. *(They exchange several "fishie" kisses and then he kisses her long and seriously, Stephen and Jerry looking on. Then Cal and Stephen head off the same way Lin exited, opposite the patio.)*

Scene 4

JERRY. What's in your purse that he doesn't want you to put down your throat, up your nose, or into your veins?
EMILY. Nothin'. I mean, I got, see, these allergies and he doesn't like me to take my antihistamines 'cause they make me real kinda loggy. He doesn't like me to be loggy.
JERRY. I buy that. Because I'm new to earth. Emily, I been around virtually nothing but addicts of one sort or another the last decade. You wanna play "Guess My Addiction?" What was the medication you both took awhile ago?
EMILY. Vitamins.
JERRY. What he gave you looked like some kinda antibiotic. What's in your purse, I'd guess from your behavior, is maybe a little cocaine.
EMILY. I think we should just work on a scene now. Help me do our first scene, about the painting, okay?
JERRY. No, not that one. The one that starts on page twenty-seven. We'll just read through it once. Can you see without your glasses?
EMILY. Oh, I don't need 'em at all. I just wear 'em so I won't look like what everyone thinks I am. *(She takes the glasses*

off, puts them aside. She finds the scene.) Oh. Gee. Don't ya think this scene's kinda.... Ya think we should do maybe a different one?

JERRY. No. This one.

EMILY. *(A beat.)* Okay. *(She invents a "door," opens it, and enters, beginning the scene with just a touch of clichéd "porn queen" sexuality. Jerry does the scene from memory.)*

"CATHERINE". "A lotta guys are real slobs. This is nice, you keep your atarpment — you keep your tapart — your a*part*ment ..." Okay, wait, I'm starting over, okay?

JERRY. Relax. You don't have to work at being sexy. Be yourself. Be you. Be Emily. Not Fawn.

EMILY. Oh — okay. Emily. Emily. *(She shakes herself out, tries to get loose, starts over, doing it essentially the same way. As "Catherine":)* "A lotta guys are real slobs. This is nice, you keep your a*part*ment very nice. Can I take my tejik, my kajet.... Your a*part*ment very nice. Can I take my *jacket* off?"

"JOSH". "Sure, please."

"CATHERINE". "'Please?' I don't want you to get the wrong idea. Guys often think if you take your *jacket* off, it's an imitation — an in*ti*mation — an *invitation* to" — *(Emily breaks out, dumps the script, starts away.)* Oh, gee, God, I'm so terrible!

JERRY. No, you're not.

EMILY. I'm so crappy and awful and ... and *crappy!*

JERRY. I said you're —

EMILY. Ya can't give a stupid person a smart person to play.

JERRY. Emily —

EMILY. I'm such a hammerhead, I can't even read!

JERRY. Hey, hey! Miss! Come back here! Come on! *(She returns.)* Now, are you just nervous because you're afraid Cal's got the trees bugged or do you have some kind of reading problem?

EMILY. I have some kind of *moron* problem!

JERRY. Look at me, Emily. Read my eyes. *(She does.)* You're not terrible and you're not a moron.

EMILY. I am too!

JERRY. No, you're not.

EMILY. Am!
JERRY. Not!
EMILY. Am!
JERRY. Not! *(This is repeated several more times ... until they laugh at the childishness of the exchange.)* It's not you. It's the script. My fault. She shouldn't say anything suggestive. Bad writing. We'll rewrite, we'll fix it. Let's just relax a minute, whudduya say? Do a little yoga, have a little chat. For instance, no big deal, but I can't help wondering just how you met his divinity, the Rev. Calvin Rhodes. *(She isn't forthcoming with a response.)* Church social? *(She shakes her head.)* Confessional booth?
EMILY. His religion, they don't have confession.
JERRY. Bar Mitzvah?
EMILY. What's that?
JERRY. A Jewish praying and eating event.
EMILY. I'm not Jewish.
JERRY. Never would've guessed.
EMILY. Calvin was only kidding.
JERRY. Calvin wasn't kidding, Calvin was goading, but I didn't bite because I was being cool; perhaps you noticed. So where'd ya meet? Simple question. Hell, as far as I'm concerned you can lie if you want to. I just want you to relax.
EMILY. I'm relaxed, we can try the scene again.
JERRY. But now I'm tense. Why, today, Emily, parts of me incapable of tenseness are tense. *(He smiles. So does she.)*
EMILY. I was selling men's shirts and ties outside the Port Authority bus station in New York City and Cal comes up and wants a striped shirt to go with a chalk stripe suit, he says. But it was a trick; he was really tryin' to get me away from these two whackos I was workin' for that were kinda holdin' me prisoner in their apartment.
JERRY. So he rescued you from the street and promoted you to porn princess.
EMILY. Well, there are some parts in between.
JERRY. Do a lotta the runaways he takes off the street end up in pornographic movies?
EMILY. No. He helps a lotta kids, Jerry.

JERRY. How?

EMILY. He talks to 'em and gets 'em jobs or lotsa times he makes 'em go home to their moms.

JERRY. Who's Carlos?

EMILY. A kinda businessman that Calvin sorta works for.

JERRY. He putting up Cal's share of the movie money?

EMILY. I think.

JERRY. So, this project is important to Cal, isn't it? He sees my script as *his* way out too, doesn't he?

EMILY. Can I make a suggestion?

JERRY. Is this called changing the subject?

EMILY. I think you should definitely keep the title. *Catherine Liberty.*

JERRY. Why?

EMILY. You can't tell Calvin. Do you promise?

JERRY. I promise.

EMILY. I went to the library one day, by myself, and I looked up the painting and this writer said the painter, that Delacroix, ya know, he didn't know whether ... he was unsure about his sexual preference. So I thought maybe Liberty's breasts are exposed because she scares him — women do, I mean — and so, unconsciously, he could humiliate her by putting her in front of all those guys half naked, not carrying a weapon like the guys, but only that — you know, the guys' flag-thing.

JERRY. Their standard.

EMILY. Yeah. And so I understood a lot about what you felt maybe about Catherine and Josh and that it was ... well, it was a really good title and the discussion they have about the painting's pretty important. *(A beat.)* Is what I just said really dumb?

JERRY. No. What you just said reconfirmed for me what I've written is right. I was sitting in there wondering if I should lose all that Delacroix stuff. Thank you very much.

EMILY. Really?

JERRY. Yes.

EMILY. You swear?

JERRY. I swear.

EMILY. Gosh, that's just so nice. I mean usually as soon as guys know who I am and what I've done and that I've got a tenth grade education, they don't take me very seriously.
JERRY. Not many women take me seriously.
EMILY. People really like to pigeonhole people, ya ever notice that?
JERRY. Nope, never did.
EMILY. Ya haven't?
JERRY. I'm kidding.
EMILY. That's nice too. Nobody kids me either unless it's really mean. *(A beat: Eyes locked together. She breaks away.)* God, I wish I had me a trailer on a river. Grill a T-bone outside on a dealie like that. One a those food chopper things that you can shoestring up some 'taters for a guy ya really like. Go in the super market and know the produce guy by name. "Hey, Armando, how's the Boston Bibb lettuce today — you recommend it?" Except I'll probably never have a place like this 'cause Calvin, he wants to be President of Paramount Pictures, and we'll probably end up livin' some place like Beverly Hills.... You respect women, don't ya?
JERRY. I got no respect for men, so I'm tryin' women.
EMILY. What about Mrs. Ryder?
JERRY. That's a problem, Emily. The only thing I can think to say to you on that subject is she's a really interesting Gook.
EMILY. Did you have to kill anyone in Vietnam?
JERRY. Yeah, I was required to do that.
EMILY. Who'd you have to kill?
JERRY. Oh, ya know, a nice assortment of slant-eyed individuals of various ages and sexes.
EMILY. Don't look at me like that.
JERRY. Like how?
EMILY. Like that. It's not good. Okay?
JERRY. I have an idea.
EMILY. What?
JERRY. Let's go inside and work on the scene.
EMILY. We're too tense.
JERRY. It's a tense scene. I should have realized from the beginning that precisely what it needs is a lotta tension be-

tween the two participants. Help me up the ramp. *(She pushes him up the ramp.)* All right, ready to resurrect the emotionally dead?
EMILY. Okay. But one thing. This is real, real awful important to Calvin *and* to me.
JERRY. Oh, it's real, real awful important to me too, Emily, have no doubt about that.
EMILY. Okay. So you gotta make me better. *(As music rises, he holds out a fist to her. She taps his fist with hers as the lights fade to half light and we watch Emily and Jerry move into position to rehearse. Lin — presumably having returned during this interim from her walk — enters from the bedroom with a book and notebook and highlighter; she sits on the couch to study ... and to take in the rehearsal.)*

Scene 5

An hour later. The rehearsal and the studying continue silently within. At the edge of the stage: Stephen and Cal return from fishing. During the following, Stephen will put the fishing gear away.

CAL. The bottom line, Steve, is you accept the arrangement I've offered and I promise you'll live a life of extraordinary and diverse gluttony — culinary, sexual, residential, sartorial, tonsorial, automotive — the gamut of indulgences.
STEPHEN. I understand what you're offerin', Pastor Cal, and I'd be lyin' if I didn't admit there's an appeal, but Jerry's my partner and my friend. You're askin' me to hurt him.
CAL. That's a gross over-simplification — hurt someone, not hurt someone. I'm asking you to make an enlightened business decision.
STEPHEN. Yeah, okay, I'll think about it, I will, but you gotta do like you said and really consider lettin' him —
CAL. Do you know how many sermons I've preached in my twelve years as a minister?

STEPHEN. I don't know — a lot, hundreds, I 'spose.

CAL. One. Twelve years ago. By the end of that first and only sermon, I realized I despised the people I was talking to for being so weak as to need me. Do you know how unattractive the ordinary, decent, passive man is — not only to himself, but to those he would impress and attract?

STEPHEN. I hear what you're sayin', but just let me talk to Jerry ... let me talk to him, and you give him a chance to show ya what he —

CAL. Have the pluck, Stephen, to divest yourself of what holds you back and stand with me. Proverbs XXIV: "A man cannot go upon hot coals and his feet not be burned." *(Cal kisses Stephen on the forehead and then leaves Stephen to follow him into the trailer.)*

Scene 6

CAL. *(Entering.)* Harriet, I'm home!

EMILY. Hi. How many fish did you catch?

CAL. How many do you think?

EMILY. Seven.

CAL. Very close.

EMILY. How many?

CAL. None.

EMILY. Ya didn't catch *any*thing?

CAL. "Didn't catch anything?" Didn't *see* anything. Not with gills anyway. An abundance of soda pop cans, fast food receptacles, and used condoms, but nary a fish. Well, what's holdin' up the show here, let's see this scene. Yawl ready, Jerry?

JERRY. Yep.

EMILY. Is it okay, Mrs. Ryder, if I use the kitchen?

LIN. Yes, fine. *(She indicates to Stephen that she's going in the bedroom with her books.)*

STEPHEN. Na, come on, please, watch the scene, huh — stay. *(A beat ... and Lin stays. Emily talks to herself.)*

EMILY. Be loose, be loose. Loose lips, loose lips. Emily Emily Emily Emily ... *(She fibrillates her lips, takes several deep breaths ... and plays the scene as she and Jerry rehearsed it, carrying the script at first, then putting it down to glance at it a time or two, then finally working without it altogether. She is, in fact, quite good and we can see what made Jerry believe in her ability to play the role. She nibbles on a carrot.)*
"CATHERINE". "Most guys are real slobs. You keep your apartment very nice."
"JOSH". "Na, I just cleaned it for the occasion; it usually looks like a landfill."
"CATHERINE". "Well, I'm glad I inspired you to clean the place ... though I wasn't gonna come."
"JOSH". "I'm surprised. Usually, I have to bar the door to keep women out."
"CATHERINE". "I just didn't want you to think if I came it meant anything other than neighborly friendliness. I don't mean that to sound unkind."
"JOSH". "Just sounds straight forward."
"CATHERINE". "You like people to be straight forward with you?"
"JOSH". "Not particularly, no. You?"
"CATHERINE". "Hell no. Okay, so where's your oregano?"
"JOSH". "Whatever I have's in that cupboard there.
"CATHERINE". I see a sock and some Tang."
"JOSH". "Isn't Tang a spice?
"CATHERINE". "Tang on fettucini — whudduya think?"
"JOSH". "Why do you let that guy beat you up?
"CATHERINE". "Isn't that a coffee and desert question?"
"JOSH". "Why?"
"CATHERINE". "Well, I guess I'm either really misguided or I must think that's what I deserve."
"JOSH". "I'm thinking about killing him."
"CATHERINE". "Can I watch?"
"JOSH". "Sure."
"CATHERINE". "I'm kidding."
"JOSH". "I'm not."
"CATHERINE". "He had a very difficult childhood."

"JOSH". "Then now I sympathize with him."
"CATHERINE". "I have an idea — let's change the subject."
"JOSH". "I dream of you. Some of them have to do with food — going shopping together, cooking together. But most of them have a sexual orientation and center on consumption. Lotta carrots. Occasionally cucumbers. Yellow squash in season."
"CATHERINE". "Josh, I can be your friend — though probably not a very good one — but I'm not interested in a sexual relationship with you."
"JOSH". "You have to be interested in a sexual relationship with me, or I'm gonna take you by force." *(He grabs her violently.)*
"CATHERINE". "Tell me if this makes sense to you, okay? You ask me how I can let one guy beat me up and then you beat me up?"
"JOSH". "Just one taste." *(He licks her imprisoned face.)*
"CATHERINE". "Oh Jesus, that's nauseating! Wipe that off!"
"JOSH". "Mouths are where the power is. A man can have no feeling in most of his body and life, but if he's got a mouth and a tongue, he's got power."
"CATHERINE". "That's very poetic, but you're hurting me and that was spit." *(He licks her again.)* "Oh, for Godsake, that's not the way to do this — slurping a person like a popsicle."
"JOSH". "How should I do it?"
"CATHERINE". "What if I show you?"
"JOSH". "What if you do?"
"CATHERINE". "Then I'm either a liar or a tease."
"JOSH". "Either way I'm willing to be taken advantage of." *(He lets her go.)*
"CATHERINE". "One taste."
"JOSH". "Okay."
"CATHERINE". "Vegetables."
"JOSH". "Yeah." *(She puts the carrot in his mouth.)*
"CATHERINE". "Tease. Come on, play, titillate." *(He sort of pokes the carrot at her face.)* "What am I, a piece of wood — don't whomp me with it. You should remember how to do

this, you used to be a man." *(He has to adjust his position, relock his chair; then he begins to tease her gently with the carrot, putting it to her lips then pulling it away as she starts to take it. Then he lets her take it and she bites a piece off. So does he ... and they chew their way to each other's mouths and kiss, mouths full of carrot. When the kiss persists ...)*

CAL. Well, that's fine, thank you very much. *(But Jerry doesn't let Emily go ... and Cal hurtles at them, yanks them apart.)* I said that's enough.

EMILY. The scene's not over yet, Calvin.

CAL. I've read the script, I know where the scene goes. My opinion, Jerry, is that far more prepossessing than your desire to be the Spielberg of pornography is your desire to get laid.

JERRY. That simple, huh? Crippled guy wants free sex.

CAL. And good Lord, look what you did to her! You've got her posturing and gesticulating and acting!

JERRY. Oh no, buddy, no ya don't. You just can't stand the fact that I proved I could do what I said I could do.

CAL. Let's go, Emily.

EMILY. But you said —

CAL. Right now, please.

EMILY. *Calvin!*

CAL. Yes ... *Fawn?*

EMILY. *You ...*

CAL. Yes — I what? I what ... *Fawn?* You have something to say to me? *(Emily hurriedly gets her things together.)*

STEPHEN. Cal, you asked them to do a scene, so it doesn't seem fair to —

CAL. *(To Stephen.)* You and your friend wanna make a movie with Fawn Sierra, then you gotta make a movie with the Rev. Calvin Rhodes, and you make a movie with the Rev. Calvin Rhodes, you make it one way: his. Decide by tomorrow morning what you want to do, gentlemen. Steve, we'll see you at the screening tonight. *(Cal and Emily are out the door.)*

JERRY. *(After them.) I don't need till tomorrow morning. I can tell ya right now! You can go straight to hell!*

STEPHEN. Goddamn you people! Goddamn all of yawl! *Stephen can barely contain his rage. He storms off-stage to the bed-*

room. Jerry wheels to the TV, snaps it on. Inaugural festivities come on and up — Walter Cronkite reporting on the curses of Iranian students as the hostages departed followed quickly by his intro of the Mormon Tabernacle Choir singing the last chorus of "The Battle Hymn of the Republic" as the Reagan inaugural parade ends.)

LIN. Let it be over with them, Jerry. There is someone who will help you get the movie made the way it should be made.

JERRY. *Chi ma may!* [Lo ma may!] (Fuck you!)

LIN. *Mat day!* [Muck yi!] (You're crazy, you're beneath me!)

JERRY. *Cho de!* [Jo-day!] (Your mother is a dog!)

LIN. *Mat day!* [Muck yi.) *(Outside, during the above: Emily sneaks a quick snort of cocaine from a small vial in her purse before Cal is completely down the ramp. He lets her twist in the wind until the beat above finishes.)*

CAL. To what lengths did you go in rehearsing that scene, Emily? *(Cal suddenly strikes Emily a vicious blow across the face.)* Where did that vegetable go when it left your mouth?

EMILY. We didn't even do the carrot when we were practicing, Calvin. *(Cal punches her in the stomach; she collapses against the picnic table.)*

CAL. Where did your mouth go when that vegetable went elsewhere? *(He yanks Emily around, lands on her, and starts to choke her with the strap from her purse.)* How can I touch you after you've been defiled by that cripple? How can I possibly purge you of his saliva and fingers and organs? I don't lose women to other men, Emily. I give women up, I give women away, on occasion I have one killed ... *(He yanks her to her feet by her hair, twists it so she's doubled over in pain, and shoves her off-stage. A beat and ...)* ... but I don't lose them to other men. *(He stands a moment, takes a cigar out.)* Have you no sense whatsoever of appropriate Christian behavior? *(He pops the cigar in his mouth and follows her as "The Battle Hymn of the Republic" swells to its stirring conclusion and the stage goes dark.)*

ACT TWO

Scene 1

Later that night. Lin plays her own composition on the electric piano. Cal, dressed in non-clerical garb, crosses the patio and enters soundlessly behind her. After several moments, Lin senses someone and turns.

CAL. Very nice indeed. Very ... tuneful.
LIN. Thank you.
CAL. I assume that's the love theme the boys hope to convince you to let them use in the movie.
LIN. It's just something I wrote for myself. I didn't hear you come in.
CAL. Didn't you?
LIN. No, I didn't. You look quite different.
CAL. Don't like to scare off the movie-goers with my clerical garb. We missed you at the screening.
LIN. I don't go there.
CAL. You don't go there, but you take the money from those who do go there.
LIN. Yes. Where are the others?
CAL. Jerry's coming in his van. Emily had a lengthy line of autograph seekers, Steve had patrons and journalists to stroke, and I thought he and Emily ought to have a little time alone to get to know each other.... I'm glad to find you here alone.
LIN. Why?
CAL. We're going to be seeing a lot of each other through the next weeks. I want you to like me.
LIN. That's not possible.
CAL. Perhaps I'm dense, but I don't see that I've done anything to merit your disrespect at this juncture, Mrs. Ryder. Except, perhaps, to make a few observations you found threat-

ening.

LIN. I didn't like the remarks. I didn't find them threatening.

CAL. Then what's the problem?

LIN. I just intuit that you are like an onion.

CAL. You intuit I'm an onion.

LIN. I think a person could peel away layer after layer, and to the very core the person would discover you are not a good man.

CAL. Well, in your culture it may be appropriate to damn people for what you intuit they are; in ours, however, we judge people on the basis of their actions.

LIN. Excuse me, I'm going to wait outside.

CAL. Good gracious! And then what? When the others arrive, come back inside to serve us dinner in festering, submissive silence? What's the point? I'll wait outside, you can lock the door; when the others return, you explain to your one-armed husband and his paraplegic friend why I'm in exile. That I suggested you're enamored of your husband's friend. That I flirted with you and made unthreatening remarks. That I am an onion. Shall I go outside?

LIN. Yes, please, it's a nice night, I would prefer that.

CAL. Well, I think that's unfair; therefore, I won't do it. To the contrary, I'm going to stay right here and charm you into affording me the same chance to alter your view of me that I'm willing to offer you. *(He smiles his smile.)*

LIN. When you've made some money, you really ought to get better caps put on your teeth.

CAL. Caps? What caps?

LIN. My father was a dentist. You have caps on at least all your visible upper teeth. If you expect that smile to work, I would seriously consider some good prosthetic dentistry. *(A beat.)* When you arrived this afternoon, you knew I wasn't Latina.

CAL. Did I?

LIN. I think you did.

CAL. Well, people are prone to think what they will.

LIN. Did you know I wasn't Latina?

CAL. Yes, I knew that.
LIN. Why did you do that?
CAL. Why do you think I did that?
LIN. I don't know, except I sensed at that moment you were not here on a mission of kindness.
CAL. Ah, that oriental intuition again then.
LIN. I would like to ask you something else.
CAL. I would love you to ask me something else.
LIN. How can you be a man of God, truly, and still promote what Emily does?
CAL. Well, Emily, as it happens, is a very, very bad child. I'm encouraging her to do the bad things she does so well in the hope of saving other lost and deviant children who aren't yet irredeemable, as I fear she is. In exchange, I'm going to produce this film and permit her to become her dream: the American icon, a motion picture star.
LIN. If you think I believe for a moment that you have the remotest concern for children, you're mistaken.
CAL. The mistake, then, would be yours. Half of every penny I take in goes to the Rhodes Foundation.
LIN. As for Emily, you didn't think she could do the role until you saw what Jerry accomplished with her in an hour.
CAL. He did nothing with her.
LIN. He did a lot with her.
CAL. Nothing.
LIN. I was here. I watched. I don't want to know this anymore than you do, but I know he's better than I want him to be. I know that what he's written could actually be good if he didn't think he had no choice left but to exploit the very worst in himself by getting you to make this movie.
CAL. I am amused by your thinking, Mrs. Ryder, and by your condemnation of me. You have children and you feed and clothe them from the profits from that porno theater, do you not?
LIN. Stephen provides a service; he does not show any movies with violence toward women or that debase them.
CAL. How do you know that if you don't go there?
LIN. He tells me, I believe him.

CAL. He's a saint and you have absolved yourself of any taint. Nice.
LIN. No, we are dirty. I am so dirty. I know these defenses are feeble.
CAL. So, get out.
LIN. We're trying! We are going to school! We want to!
CAL. It's so difficult to know where the line is when one stops being tainted and becomes virulent contagion itself. Isn't it? *(This is so difficult for Lin, not just him, his presence here with her, but her internal conflicts ...)*
LIN. Yes!
CAL. I had begun to think you were without flaw, Mrs. Ryder. One of those wonderfully pure minority individuals who are periodically thrust at us as the suffering ideal of human equanimity and decorum.
LIN. I just know there is a difference between what you are offering and what they — what we — are seeking.
CAL. My, I like your spunk, Mrs. Ryder. It's abundantly clear where the finer points of Catherine's character come from. I saw you mouthing the lines with Emily. My God, I find you appealing.
LIN. I don't want you to talk to me like this.
CAL. Then by all means I'll stop. Your husband tells me you're in the thesis year of your Masters degree in the Horticulture program here. What does one grow up to be with a graduate degree in horticulture?
LIN. I'm specializing in hydroponics.
CAL. Hydroponics.
LIN. It's a relatively new field.
CAL. Don't tell me. "Hydro"–meaning water, of course. "Ponics," meaning ... Ponics, pon, pon, ponics ...
LIN. It has to do with —
CAL. I asked you not to tell me. I know "pon," I know "pon." Took a Linguistics course once with a ferocious etymological bent ... "Pon, pon, pon." "Hydro" is Greek, so it would naturally follow that "pon" ... Goddamn it! *(A beat ... and he peers into the pot on the stove into which he spat earlier.)* Ah, the effluvium of coconut milk — a smell that brings back

all the labyrinthine memories of childhood. I used to take a crabclaw hammer to a coconut in my driveway, would pretend it was the skull of my beloved father; would husk it, punch out the eyes with a screwdriver, suck down the milk, smash the nut on the concrete, and chew out the flesh in a paroxysm of primal vengeance. *(Cal takes a long stemmed herb out of the glass in which Lin has a bunch soaking and sniffs a stalk.)* Mm — what's this?

LIN. It's Called lemon grass.

CAL. Though I believe it's official name is citronella. We must be having a dish or two from Thailand — very promising. I hate to plead for acceptance, Mrs. Ryder, but I do think if you bothered to get to know me, you'd find I am at the very least a veritable refuse heap of useless information and erudition. *(A beat.)* You're thinking you know me quite well enough now, thank you, aren't you? Yes, I think you are. But if I know nothing else in life, Mrs. Ryder, I know this: You may think you know me but, believe me, you don't. Because you see, Mrs. Ryder, I don't compute.

LIN. Really?

CAL. What if I told you, for instance, I had asthma until I was fifteen, then colitis followed by a duodenal ulcer, but that the achievement of the appellation "reverend" before my name made me hale and whole and able to withstand the very sort of prejudice I've met here today? What if I told you my beloved father made me practice lay-ups right-handed and left-handed for hours on end in junior high school, but never impressed on me the necessity to really learn to dribble well enough left-handed to drive to my left? What if I told you that I filled out an application to the American Nazi Party when I was in college, but put the wrong postage on it and got it back and never remailed it because I didn't want to stand in line at the post office to get the correct postage? What if I told you that earlier today I stood right here and spat in that pot with its simmering sauce of coconut milk and cilantro? If I told you those things or things like those things, you might begin to assume that I do compute, but that would make you wrong.... So your husband tells me you went to school at the Sorbonne in Paris. *Eh bien, dites-moi, dites-moi tout sur vous, racontez-mois votre vie.* [Well, tell me, tell me everything about you, tell me your life.] *(When she doesn't respond.)* Please. What else do we have to do while we await the return of our loved ones? I'm not going to go outside, are you? *Racontez-mois votre vie, si vous plait.*

LIN. I really don't care to talk about myself.

CAL. *Ecoutez, parlons encore un peu. Qu'en dites-vous?* [Come on, let's have some fun. Want to?] *(He smiles, then remembering what she said about his teeth, he kills the smile. He sits at the piano and plays the first two bars of Lin's love theme.)* A love theme written for oneself seems a very lonely notion. *My* intuition tells me that we're not so different ... *(He turns to stare at her ...)* ... but if you don't want to share your history with me, by all means don't. Leave me to the implications your husband has made about your past.

LIN. What implications?

CAL. He led me to believe, as I suspected, of course, that you were a prostitute in Saigon; out of whatever lunacy makes for such guilt, he brought you and your two illegitimate children to America and the opulence of this trailer — or mobile home, I'm sure you'd prefer I call it.

LIN. Stephen would not imply such things.

CAL. And yet he did.

LIN. Never.

CAL. Then you're blind to how desperately your husband wants to charm *me.*

LIN. My father was a dentist, and I grew up in Paris and attended the Sorbonne.

CAL. Of course you did. And then in a burst of rejuvenated patriotism you returned to the homeland, there to attend wounded G.I.s.

LIN. I'm going to tell you the truth and I want you to hear it clearly: I met a young dentist in Paris through my father — he also was an expatriate Vietnamese. Together we returned to Vietnam in 1970. In 1972 I was pregnant with our second child. My husband was killed in a rocket attack on the dental clinic where we worked, I was wounded in the abdomen. I swore that if my baby survived the rip in my belly, I would live a good and decent life in this terrible and inhospitable world. In the hospital in Saigon, while I was recovering and awaiting my labor, I started working with wounded servicemen. I met Stephen there. That the "good and decent life" I swore myself to is coming with great difficulty has not dissuaded me from pursuing that promise. *That* is the truth.

CAL. Certainly sounds plausible when you say it.

LIN. It makes no difference to me whether you believe me or not.

CAL. Then why tell me with such adamant and self-righteous conviction?

LIN. I'm going outside. *(She heads for the door, but Cal cuts her off.)*

CAL. Isn't it time to cut out all this polite badinage, Mrs. Ryder? Why don't we get to the point.

LIN. Which is what?

CAL. Given your keen observational skills and your willingness to share them with me, are you or are you not prepared to act on the way you were looking at me all afternoon?

LIN. What does that mean?

CAL. I believe you find me just as perversely attractive as I find you. Two intrinsically virtuous human beings battling the allure of evil.

LIN. You're crazy.

CAL. Oh, I don't think so. Understand: whatever you are, whore or aristocrat, it doesn't matter; our desire to rise from the morass, our aloneness and isolation, are the same. Now don't say anything, just listen a moment. I want you to leave here with me. The movie business isn't my only option. Come away with me, meet some people, visit some cathedrals, eat some pompano. We'll lie down together somewhere where it's safe and I'll run my tongue across your almond eyes and massage your corneas with my tongue. Do you like sex? Perhaps it's been so long since you've been touched in a creative manner, you've forgotten. Was the carrot your idea? Do you fantasize about that sort of playfulness? *(He reaches a hand for her; she repels it.)*

LIN. Don't touch me.

CAL. I'd like you to indulge me. I'll only touch that place, that little indentation in your cheek, that shadow there. It has always been my gift to know what people want better than they; let what's inside come to me, I'll protect you from its fury. *(He reaches ... and she retreats.)*

LIN. I don't want you to touch me. Don't touch me.

CAL. The thing is, though, Mrs. Ryder, in the end I touch what I care to touch — especially what pretends to be repelled by me. *(A beat. From the road Jerry sounds his horn.)*

LIN. That's Jerry. Could you help him up the ramp?

CAL. No. But do you know what I would like to do at this juncture? I'd like to see the scars on your abdomen from where you were wounded in the service of democracy. *(She tries to go around him. He grabs her. She tries to pull free. He's much too strong.)*

LIN. I told you not to touch me. You have no right to touch me. *(He jams her arm up behind her back, between her shoulders; she gives up a little cry.)*

CAL. You say you were wounded. I'd like to see for myself. You could yell for help. Your friend Jerry could wheelchair to your rescue. Are you going to show me your scars, Mrs. Ryder? *(In a flash he has his hand under her blouse and down the front of her skirt. She struggles. He stills her by again violently jamming her arm upward.)*

LIN. Don't do this, please don't do this.

CAL. What would it cost, you figure, to have good caps put on my teeth? Coupla thousand? Gotta figure in the rate of inflation — what's it gonna be this year, ya figure? What was it last year — over twelve percent, wasn't it? *(He finds the scar across her abdomen.)* Oh my, my, that's some ferocious undulating scar. *(She tries to break away. He twists her powerfully onto the couch, imprisoning her there, his hand still at her belly. She hangs over his knees like a rag doll, her head practically dragging the floor.)* You know that American auto sales fell twenty percent this year? People aren't buying American, they're buying Jap and Kraut. Your people make a decent car? A Gookmobile? Though come to think of it, I don't know one person who drives a Vietnamese car. I'm not sure you people manufacture anything exportable, except maybe those incredible penicillin resistant strains of venereal disease. *(During the above his hand has moved downward ... and now Lin cries out and we must assume that he has intruded his fingers into her.)* You try being a man of God in a world like this. You try saving the contemporary soul. Try saving anything. Try saving enough money to buy a decent pair of athletic shoes. *(He takes his hand out of her skirt, stares at his fingers. She lies limp across his knees.)* You have a helluva deal working here, don't you? If I make this movie with your husband and his psychotic friend, you know they're gone, you're rid of both of them; they're off in search of celebrity and fortune, and you and your children end up with a beautiful hunk of land on a river, half a house, no more porno dilemmas, and a Masters degree in Hydroponics. You can get on, finally, to living that "good and decent life in this inhospitable world." *(He takes his "taste," running his tongue along her neck and cheek ... then turns her loose, pushes her away from him. She scrambles to her feet.)* Helluva deal. Thanks to me. *N'est-ce pas? (He puts the fingers that were inside of her to his lips. And Lin explodes, comes at his eyes with her fingers. He knocks her away. She comes at him again, tries to kick him in the groin. He knocks her away. Then she leaps at him, landing a blow in his stomach that he feels. He takes her to the floor, locks her arms across his knees, hyper-extending them, threatening to dislocate them with a thrust. Outside: Jerry appears.)*

JERRY. Yo — hey, Lin, ya wanna gimme a hand out here, please!

CAL. Terrible to live an entire life in which you have no power over anyone, isn't it? I can't imagine how unspeakable that must be. *(Cal turns Lin loose and walks away from her. Again, she scrambles to her feet. They stare at each other.)*

Scene 2

... and then Lin goes out of the trailer, will put the ramp over the stairs and help Jerry up and in during the following. In the meantime: Cal goes quickly to the bookshelf, grabs a dictionary, and looks up "hydroponics."

JERRY. You hear me calling?
LIN. I'm here, Jerry.
JERRY. You think I'd call you if I didn't have to?
LIN. No.
JERRY. He in there?
LIN. Yes.
JERRY. What's the matter? What's wrong? *(She shakes her head.)* Help me in, please.
CAL. *(In the dictionary.)* "Hoyden." *(Flips couple of pages.)* "Hurtleberry." *(Flips couple of pages.)* "Hydrogenate. Hydrophyte. Hydroplane. Hydro*ponics!*" *(He reads quickly, slams the dictionary shut, stows it, and sits at the piano, where he plays Tchaikovsky's "Piano Concerto Number One" ... as Lin helps Jerry up the ramp and into the trailer. During the following, Lin goes onto the patio, alone there to try to deal with what's happened and to wait for Stephen.)*
JERRY. *(At Cal.)* Hey!
CAL. Jer, what'd ya think? Incredible turnout, huh? I mean, I was amazed. Nice to see all those college boys and girls with a nose for the *recherché* [exotic].
JERRY. How come you had her standing out there in the lobby naked?
CAL. I frankly don't like the tone of voice with which you asked that question, Jerry.
JERRY. Just answer my question!
CAL. I'm not gonna answer the question, until you ask it in a manner I find suitably civil. *(Jerry yanks Cal's hands off the keyboard.)*
JERRY. How could you have her standing —
CAL. I'm telling you, Jer, don't try to bully me; it's just not

an effective way to deal with me. You have a question to ask me, ask it in an appropriate manner and I'll be only too happy to consider an answer.

JERRY. At the theater tonight ...

CAL. Good. Yes?

JERRY. ... why were people greeted by Emily with no clothes on?

CAL. Just a little something I thought I'd do for the occasion. But that wasn't Emily. Who was that, Jerry? That was Fawn Sierra, who has become a celebrity of no small magnitude, and not because of her poetry, her political views, or her fish sticks.

JERRY. They can see her totally naked on the screen.

CAL. Not quite the same as seeing her unclad in person.

JERRY. She was humiliated.

CAL. Oh, I don't think so.

JERRY. She was humiliated.

CAL. Did she tell you that?

JERRY. Oh come on, man, she didn't have to tell me.

CAL. In other words, you divined it with your own internal antennae.

JERRY. Oh man, you got the Devil's tongue, don't you, huh?

CAL. Oh, I don't know that I'd go that far, Jerry. *(Jerry grabs Cal.)* Don't do that, Jerry.

JERRY. And what about the bruises on her arms that you could see through the body make-up? *(Cal breaks free.)*

CAL. She's also got a boil right in the crevasse below her left buttock. What's the point?

JERRY. You hit her? *(Jerry pursues Cal. Sound of Stephen's Volkswagen horn. Lin looks off; waits.)*

CAL. Don't chase me, Jerry. I don't enjoy being chased.

JERRY. Then stand still and answer my question. Do you hit her?

CAL. There is no violence in *No End In Sight,* Jerry, precisely because I abhor physical violence, which is precisely why I won't stand still. If I stand still, I'll be forced to hurt you.

JERRY. Let's find out who'll hurt who. Come on, damn it,

fight me like a man. *(Jerry pursues Cal again.)*

CAL. Sure, Jer, like men, wanna fight like men? *(Cal suddenly plants himself and utterly explodes, hitting Jerry so hard in the shoulder that he knocks Jerry over in his wheelchair. Jerry lies in a heap. Hearing the crash, Lin hurries to the door. Cal dumps Jerry out of the wheelchair and gets in himself, gives it a try.)*

JERRY. Help me up.

CAL. Why? You're an independent kinda guy. Soldier, actor, filmmaker. *(When Cal doesn't help him up, Lin comes to Jerry's aid.)*

JERRY. Don't touch me! *(She backs off.)*

CAL. Ya notice, Jerry, for a man who really seems to be incredibly sensitive to the way women are mistreated by guys like me, you got a little problem with Mrs. Ryder here. And believe me, it didn't take Emily telling me you referred to Missy Rydah heah as a Gook for me to recognize that. So she's Vietnamese; she's not one of theirs, she's one of ours. Isn't that right, Missy Rydah? *(Cal shoots the wheelchair at Jerry. Jerry positions the chair, locks it down, moves his legs into position, tries to lift himself.)* Now, are you in this or are you out, Jerry? If you're out, fine; but if you're in, tend to the business of writing and keep your nose out of the business of my relationship with Emily. *(The shoulder in which Cal blasted him won't hold Jerry's weight and he can't lift himself alone. Finally, Lin steps close again.)*

LIN. Let me help you, Jerry.

JERRY. *(A beat.)* Please. *(Lin puts her arms around Jerry, he puts his around her and together they get him up into the chair as Cal sits to play the first movement of Beethoven's* Moonlight Sonata. *Lin places Jerry's legs and feet properly and then starts to pull away, but he takes hold of her hand.) Chi rat tot.* [Jay rot do.] *(You're a good person.)*

LIN. *Ktiong co chi.* [Kong go chi.] (It's okay.) *(Lin goes to the door as the lights dim inside. She just misses Stephen and Emily's entrance so that she stands up on the porch for some seconds anticipating Stephen's arrival before she comes down the ramp. Through a scrim wall, the back wall of the trailer, she can always be visible to us during the times she's outside.)*

Scene 3

Stephen and Emily have entered following the last words between Jerry and Lin. Cal continues to play Moonlight Sonata *throughout.*

STEPHEN. Wait a minute, hold on a second, okay? *(He indicates the picnic table. She follows him down stage to the table.)* Na, never mind.

EMILY. What? Tell me.

STEPHEN. Just that I haven't told ya near the truth.

EMILY. Whudduya mean, what's wrong?

STEPHEN. It's more'n what I just said — my confidence in ya, how grateful I am ya wanna do our film.... Truth is, since I first saw ya in *No End In Sight* I can't think about any other woman. When Jerry did that scene with ya this afternoon, I 'bout went crazy with jealousy.

EMILY. Are you askin' me to ...

STEPHEN. No, oh Lord, I don't know ...

EMILY. I couldn't do that to Mrs. Ryder ...

STEPHEN. I know, I know it, I just ...

EMILY. And I couldn't do it anyway unless Calvin said it was ...

STEPHEN. I don't want ya to do nothin' ya don't wanna do. You're not much older'n one of my daughters ... but was that — with Jerry this afternoon — was that acting or ...

EMILY. You're not like this, Mr. Ryder. You love your wife and you got your two little girls. Don't be like everybody else.

STEPHEN. But I am like everybody else and I hate it! I don't wanna be like everybody else! I'm sick to death of being like ...

EMILY. Don't. *(Stephen pulls away.)*

STEPHEN. Okay, okay, look, nothin', nothin', don't say anything more, okay — really. *(Emily kisses Stephen on the forehead; behind them, on the ramp, Lin has seen and heard some of this. Emily heads into the trailer.)*

EMILY. Hi, Mrs. Ryder, we were just talking. *(... leaving Lin and Stephen. Stephen heads for the trailer.)*

STEPHEN. Jerry and Cal okay?

LIN. They had a fist fight.

STEPHEN. Aw no!

LIN. Stephen, I have to talk to you; he came back here —

STEPHEN. I can't talk right now, Lin; I know you're upset, I am too; later we'll talk about everything; but right now these two maniacs are on the brink of ruinin' the future and I gotta salvage it; now, just bear with me here another coupla hours, please. Two lousy hours. *(Before Lin can continue, Stephen is up the ramp and into the trailer. After a moment, Lin follows.)*

Scene 4

Lights up inside. Cal stops playing Moonlight Sonata *and ...*

CAL. Requests. Playing requests. *(... launches into a medley that includes "It's a Grand Ole Flag," the Air Force, Army, and Navy hymns, and the Notre Dame Fight Song.)*

STEPHEN. *(Interrupting.)* Cal...!

CAL. That is just one sweet little theater you got there, Steve. I mean, a lotta work went into renovating that place.

STEPHEN. I'm glad you liked it, Cal. You guys all right?

CAL. Oh, sure. We had a little talk, we're fine, eh, Jerry?

STEPHEN. Lin said you had a fist fight.

CAL. Oh, I'd say "fist fight" is a bit of an exaggeration, wouldn't you, Jer? You don't have a fist fight with a man in a wheelchair.

STEPHEN. You all right, stumper?

JERRY. Oh yeah. How 'bout you? You feeling pretty good about things, guy who has a woman standing naked in a —

CAL. I assured Jerry that Emily was only too happy to lend the evening a special significance. Weren't you, Emmie?

EMILY. I'm fine, Jerry, so please don't do anything to ruin

our chance to —

CAL. Boy, am I hungwy!

STEPHEN. We ready to eat?

LIN. A few minutes.

STEPHEN. Should I get the plates down? *(She nods. Stephen goes to the cupboards for plates, glasses, chopsticks, etc., starts to set them out.)* Chopsticks for you and Emily, Cal?

EMILY. Oh, no thanks, I've never got the hang —

CAL. Come on, Emily, when in Texas, do as the Vietnamese do — or however that saying goes.

STEPHEN. Can I get you guys a glass of wine?

CAL. Please.

STEPHEN. Emily? *(She glances at Cal, but he's not tuned to her anymore.)*

EMILY. Okay. *(Stephen pours wine as ...)*

STEPHEN. Now, you guys listen to me. Don't both of yawl realize that if this pecker poundin' contest between ya doesn't stop, the whole project's gonna go down the tubes? Now, I know that's not what you guys want, I know that, so what I guess it comes down to is which of ya is gonna be big enough to swallow some pride and put this thing back on an even keel. Look at me — both of ya! *(They do.)* Is this or ain't it important enough to rise above your petty animosities toward each other for the good a the project? *(When neither Jerry nor Cal moves.)* Hell, then let's chow down and get some sleep, stuff our dreams away and go back to our old lives. *(A beat ... and Cal offers his hand to Jerry.)*

CAL. Peace, Jerry? *(Jerry doesn't respond.)* Come on, there are no perfect marriages. How can there be among imperfect people? You want to direct your movie, you want to star in it? All right. I'll support you to Carlos. If he's amenable, we'll indemnify the completion bond ourselves.

STEPHEN. Yes!

CAL. Cal to Jerry, Cal to Jerry, come in, Jerry.

STEPHEN. Are you serious, Cal?

CAL. Absolutely.

STEPHEN. Hey, that's great, Cal, all right! Jerry did ya hear —

JERRY. So why all the fighting, why all the attacks?
CAL. Fun.
JERRY. Fun? I didn't have any fun today.
CAL. None — really? Whoa.
JERRY. I don't get it.
CAL. Don't try. Let's move forward, let's talk movie. Ya ready? Steve and I were spit-balling some ideas down at the river this afternoon. For instance: locations. Steve.
STEPHEN. Yeah, we were talkin', and we could save us beaucoup bucks by shootin' the movie right here.
JERRY. Here?
LIN. Right here where?
STEPHEN. You know, the river, the hills, the trailer.... Just hear me out a second here now, okay? We're talkin' 'bout how to make the film less claustrophobic, right? We're not tryin' to rewrite it for ya or nothin', but say Catherine's character lives in a trailer within view of Josh's trailer ...
LIN. You're not shooting here. I have children.
STEPHEN. Lin, they're in school all day. They're gone most of the day — we got no night shooting ...
LIN. Stephen, if you want to drive me out, you have only to foul the place my children live — that will do it, I promise.
STEPHEN. Lin, I'm a producer here, I got financial responsibilities. The kids won't know anything about it.
CAL. Jesus Christ, we're talking about five acres, lady — you won't even know we're here!
LIN. I'll know every day the rest of my life that you were here. *(Lin exits to the bedroom. A beat.)*
STEPHEN. If Lin doesn't want us to shoot here, we can't shoot here. *(Stephen exits after Lin.)*
CAL. *(Calling after them.)* If it's no, okay, fine, it's no; but let's hold the definitive answer until you've had the chance to speak in private. Give it that. Why don't we eat these wonderful smelling viands. Are we ready to do that, Mrs. Ryder?
STEPHEN. *(Reentering.)* It's buffet-style. Just grab a plate and load 'er up.
EMILY. Jerry, could I serve you? Are you okay?

JERRY. I'm fine.

EMILY. We're doing this movie together. Aren't you happy? See, he liked what we did, didn't you, Calvin?

CAL. My father, Jerry, owned a Cadillac agency in Miami. Drove him crazy that poor colored folks and wealthy Jewish folks were his best customers. "Ya know how come there's Nigras, son?" he'd ask me. "How come, Daddy?" "Cuz someone's gotta buy all that zebra skin upholstery I got in stock." Funny guy, my daddy. Used to have fake invoices on all his cars for the Jewish folks. "Mark 'em up for the Yids, son, so you can mark 'em down. No bargain, no buy." Jew canoes, he called 'em. Yidillacs. Became a rich man selling our most prestigious automobile to folks he despised. Perhaps there remains in me a trace of my father's racism and anti-Semitism; if so and if that in any way affected my behavior toward you today, I earnestly apologize for that too.

STEPHEN. Here's a fork, Emily.

EMILY. Oh, thank you, Mr. Ryder. I'm sorry I never learned to use chopsticks, but where I grew up there was one Chinese restaurant and it was owned by this Italian family. It was mainly like chop suey and egg rolls.

STEPHEN. I hope nobody's got any problem with spicy food.

EMILY. I don't.

STEPHEN. Cal.

CAL. No, I have no problem with spicy food. None at all.

STEPHEN. This one dish here, Emily, has coconut milk in it.

CAL. ... but it's not a dairy product.

STEPHEN. That's what I was gonna say, Cal.

CAL. I'm sorry I usurped your right to be there first with that piece of information, Steve.

EMILY. Thanks for telling me, Mr. Ryder, I really appreciate that. *(Lin returns. All eyes to her. A beat.)* Did you know Mrs. Ryder's workin' in this new farming field, Calvin, where they farm with ... in this ... in this new way?

CAL. And?

EMILY. And that's so interesting, I think. For the future.

CAL. Is this some kind of *a priori* induction you've made, Emily, to suggest there's going to *be* a future or are you merely fomenting polite conversation?

EMILY. I don't know what you mean, Calvin.

CAL. Really? Steve, how is it you chose not to opt for one of those functional prostheses with the steel pinchers so you could use that arm?

STEPHEN. Oh, you know, just kinda didn't, I guess.

CAL. Surely not a matter of vanity in a young man as forthcoming as yourself.

LIN. No different than someone who has his teeth capped, is it?

CAL. Ah-ha, I see, yes, I think I see what you're saying. Thank you for that clarification. It occurs to me, though, that a person can still chew with capped teeth. And smile. *(He smiles his smile. Lin slams a sauce pan down into the sink, goes offstage a moment for her Cowboys jacket.)*

EMILY. Oh, don't go, Mrs. Ryder. Come on, please, aren't you gonna eat?

LIN. *(Returning.) How can the two of you want to make this movie so much that you would let this man enter your lives? Don't we have to be better than this! The three of us? We are awful people, so, so weak, but don't we have limits? Jerry? Stephen, can't you see he's ... Stephen, he ... (She wants to tell Stephen what Cal did, but whirling in anger, confusion ...) ... he doesn't ... he doesn't even know what hydroponics is! (She grabs a flashlight.)*

CAL. *Hey!...* If I tell you what hydroponics is, will you let us shoot our movie here? In your trailer? On your bed? You want someone to smite me, you do it. You know they won't give up the movie unless I kill or rape someone.

STEPHEN. Aw, Cal, why would you say a thing like that? What are you trying to do here?

EMILY. Don't bet him, Mrs. Ryder. If he's willin' to bet you, then he —

CAL. What in the name of anything sensible do you think you're doing?

EMILY. I just meant you're a good bettor, Calvin —

CAL. "Hydro" — meaning water. "Ponics" — from the

Greek "pon," to work. Hydroponics. Took me awhile to figure it out, but Mrs. Ryder's going to grow plants indoors in water-based nutrients rather than soil. That's great, Mrs. Ryder. Clean vegetables and fruit and herbs. I hope it goes well for you. In case I don't see you before we go back to the hotel, thank you so much for preparing this lovely supper for us. *Au revoir.*

LIN. You looked it up in the dictionary.

CAL. When?

LIN. When I went outside to help Jerry up the ramp.

CAL. I was playing the piano.

LIN. Not at first. At first, you were looking up "hydroponics" in the dictionary.

CAL. I didn't look it up in the dictionary.

LIN. I say you did.

CAL. You really know how to hurt a person, Mrs. Ryder.

LIN. No, I don't. Because I don't exist, really, to any of you. I have no power. *(Lin starts out the door but discovers the flashlight doesn't work. She has to get fresh batteries out of the refrigerator and replace the old ones as ...)*

CAL. Your rancor startles me, Mrs. Ryder, it really does; especially after the nice things I said about your music. After I protected you and didn't disclose to your less cultured friends here that you stole that music.

STEPHEN. Cal ...

CAL. She thinks I didn't notice her homage to Saint-Saen.

STEPHEN. Cal, she didn't steal that music.

CAL. I don't think you want to make your obligatory, husbandly defense over this particular issue, Steve.

STEPHEN. I'm just telling you I know she didn't steal that music.

CAL. Not consciously, of course.

STEPHEN. Not consciously or unconsciously.

CAL. Okay, all right, fine. If we must. Here's Charles Camille Saint-Saen's "My Heart at Thy Sweet Voice" from *Samson and Delilah. (He plays a bit of it.)* And here, I believe — I may be off a note or two — is Mrs. Ryder's love theme for our film. *(He plays again the right hand notes he played ear-*

lier, which indeed represent an unadorned version of Lin's theme. He stops, looks at the others.)

STEPHEN. I don't hear the similarity.

EMILY. I don't either, Calvin.

CAL. Jerry — surely you hear it. *(A beat.)*

JERRY. No. I don't.

CAL. What'd you people grow up listening to? If you transposed the Saint-Saen this way and that, flung around some eighths and sixteenths —

LIN. Goodnight. *(The flashlight works. Lin leaves. Outside, she crosses off-stage. A beat.)*

CAL. *(Handing Emily his plate.)* Yeah. Well. I think we're gonna run along. Put this crap down the garbage disposal for me, Emily.

EMILY. Aw, Calvin — she worked real awful hard on this. Shouldn't we eat it?

CAL. Wanna eat something? How would you like to eat some ice cream? Any appeal in that suggestion?

EMILY. No.

CAL. Then dump this slop. Yours too. *(Emily does as she's told. To Stephen and Jerry.)* Breakfast at the hotel at nine. If we're not using the trailer, then we'll have to.... All right, listen, I'm really sorry if I insulted her, but.... Never mind, it's always the same — somebody impeding my way. That's what makes success so sweet. And just to keep things honest among us: These two teeth here are capped, all right? Because in the championship of the Golden Gloves when I was sixteen, after I lost on a split decision, my father hurled me into the ring post. Goodnight, thanks for a stimulating day and a wonderful screening tonight. Say thank you, Emily.

EMILY. Thank you. I really hope I'll see yawl tomorrow.

JERRY. It's no good. I can't do it.

CAL. You're mumblin', Jer. Can't do what?

JERRY. Can't do this with you. Much as I crave to. Whether to have sex with this beautiful young woman, like you said, or because I believe we could really make a helluva film ... *(A beat.)* It's over, Cal.

CAL. What's the problem? I hope to hell he's not telling

me I'm the problem here, Steve.

JERRY. Na — me, I'm the problem. I gotta get myself straight before I start preachin' about love —

CAL. Oh, this is touching. Young Jerome has experienced a true life revelation! You want Emily, Jerry? You can have her. Tonight. Here, or in a location of your choice. Standing, reclining, suspended by manacles. Because that's all this is all about between you and me, isn't it, Jer?

JERRY. If that's all it was about, I'd just go ahead and make the movie with you.

CAL. Take off your clothes, Fawn.

JERRY. Don't do it, Emily.

CAL. Denude yourself at this time, Fawn.

JERRY. Don't.

CAL. You take your clothes that I bought you off your body right now!

EMILY. He doesn't want me, Calvin.

CAL. Believe me, I know who wants you and who doesn't. This scuzball defective is practically drowning in slobber.

EMILY. Calvin, he's a nice —

CAL. You wanna eat ice cream?

EMILY. No.

CAL. Emily wanna consume a Jumbo Calvin Butterscotch Special?

EMILY. No!

CAL. Then strip! *(Jerry charges Cal in his wheelchair.)*

JERRY. Leave her alone, leave her the hell alone, and get outta here, get the goddamn hell outta here!

CAL. Don't instruct me, Jerry, who are you to instruct? Want me to put you on your ass again, like me to *really* embarrass you this time? I'm gonna give you what you want. Quit acting like you're better than you are and take it. I'm gonna give you exactly three seconds to start shuckin' those clothes, Fawn. *(Emily makes a move to start to unbutton her blouse.)*

STEPHEN. Don't, Emily.

CAL. Was that you who spoke now, Steve?

STEPHEN. Yeah.

CAL. Is that how we're gonna work together? I say one thing and you say the opposite?

STEPHEN. Maybe. Now I'm gonna ask you to take Emily and go on back to your hotel, and I'll call ya there in the mornin'.

CAL. Sure, Steve. *(To Emily.)* Why don't we amble back to the hotel. Take a baffie, play putt-putt-bang. *(To Jerry.)* Bale out on this, you make a big mistake — artistic, pecuniary, spiritual. *(He steps outside, holds the door for Emily. Emily shakes hands with Stephen ...)*

EMILY. Thanks for everything, Mr. Ryder. *(Bends to kiss Jerry's cheek.)* I'm real sorry. I think you're real handsome and real talented.

CAL. *(Coming back in.)* What'd you say?

EMILY. Nothing.

CAL. Thought I heard sound. Words. Eight words, maybe ten.

EMILY. I said good-bye.

CAL. That's only two syllables. I heard at least twelve syllables, maybe thirteen. *(Emily goes out the door and down the ramp.)* Again, merely for the record, gentlemen: 1.) Mrs. Ryder did steal that music from Saint-Saen, and 2.) I deduced, totally legitimately, the meaning of hydroponics. *(Cal smiles winningly and closes the door. Stephen stares at Jerry.)*

JERRY. We can't sell her out.

STEPHEN. Emily? We wouldn't be selling her out; we'd be giving her the chance to —

JERRY. Aw, Stevie — Lin. Lin, Stevie. *(Stephen throws himself down the hall to the bedroom as the lights dim inside.)*

Scene 5

Outside the trailer: Emily waits, frightened, wondering if Cal will do to her what he did the last time. She chants, coming at him, trying to be seductive.

EMILY. Calvie palsy walsy. Friendsy wendsy wendsy. Be nice, be nice and I'll do ya real real real good twice. *(She's on her knees before his crotch … as Lin comes in from the other side, stops, watches.)*
CAL. Nope, sorry, no effect, Emmie, you're having absolutely no effect. We'll stop at that convenience store at the end of the road. *(He grabs her abusively. Lin shines her light into the side of Cal's face.)*
LIN. Emily. *(Cal shoves Emily toward the wing and turns to face Lin.)*
CAL. Curious you didn't say anything to your husband about what happened between us. I wonder why you didn't. *(He goes off. As the following takes place inside, Lin moves up the ramp and, hearing the two men speaking, she remains outside, visible through the scrim wall throughout, listening to them.)*

Scene 6

JERRY. Hey, Stephen, I'm outta here, man.
STEPHEN. Just hold on! You just wait a minute! *(His jacket and shirt off, Stephen returns in his pants and a black T-shirt.)* This isn't about Lin. Maybe some. But it's mostly 'bout you. First ya try to drive him out, now he gives you everything and you wanna walk away because deep down inside what you really want is to fail so you can wallow in bein' a friggin' stump!
JERRY. No.
STEPHEN. I don't like you! I don't like you very damn

much at all! We coulda made it work, Jerry, I coulda protected you from him!

JERRY. Never. He would've pushed me toward failure every day.

STEPHEN. Forget him! *I* made ya believe you could do what I knew you could do, I gave ya faith in yourself, and now —

JERRY. Not really, Stevie. You helped, no question, but fact is, she did, Stevie, the oriental woman. The idiotic realization that she thought I was better than I'd allowed myself to be.... Aw, Christ, how do we get outta the slime, brother, how do we do it?

STEPHEN. We had it in our grasp! But now you can be happy, you're back to nowhere, you're just a stump in a friggin' chair! You got nothin', Jerry.

JERRY. Got me a handicapped parking sticker, brother. Park anywhere. See ya around, stumper. *(Jerry heads for the door.)*

STEPHEN. Not just yet! I want that script. I can make this deal work and I can make it work better without you to screw it up. Now I'm gonna have a contract drawn up and you're gonna sign it.

JERRY. No way.

STEPHEN. You don't wanna change your life — okay! But have the decency to get outta my way and let me change mine. I'm not gonna end up a one-handed nobody who runs a porno house! *(Emily whimpers off-stage. Lin goes off toward the sound.)*

JERRY. You got your head all the way up his ass, Stephen. You don't know who you're dealing with here.

STEPHEN. Believe me, I know who I'm dealing with and I know how to handle him. He wanted me to sell you out. I told him you were my friend, I could talk to you, that I could keep you in line. I wish to God I'd sold you out. I wish I could sell you out right now.

JERRY. Lucky for me, I guess you're not gonna have that opportunity anymore. Get outta my way.

Scene 7

Lin runs up the ramp and into the trailer.

LIN. I hear someone crying out in the trees.
STEPHEN. Somebody's cat chasin' gophers.
LIN. I know the difference between a crying woman and a cat.
JERRY. Emily? *(Stephen bursts out of the trailer.)*
STEPHEN. Which direction?
LIN. There! *(Stephen disappears into the "woods." Lin moves in that direction but stays onstage. Jerry is at the top of the ramp.)*
STEPHEN. *Emily? Here! She's here!*
LIN. *Be careful, Stephen, maybe you shouldn't pick her up.*
STEPHEN. *Too late. (Stephen comes out of the "woods" carrying Emily.)*
EMILY. Don't see me, don't see me, don't see me ...
LIN. Jerry, get a washcloth. *(Jerry goes for the washcloth. Stephen carries Emily inside, puts her on the couch.)*
EMILY. ... don't see me, don't see me, don't see me ... *(When Stephen pulls back, we can see Emily's clothing is torn, her face bloodied.)*
LIN. Can you open your mouth for me? *(Emily cries low, but opens her mouth. With the flashlight, Lin looks in her mouth, then in her ears for blood.)* The blood doesn't seem to be coming up her throat. *(Stephen covers Emily with an afghan.)* Jerry, bring me some aspirin, then call the police.
EMILY. No no no no no no no no no!
LIN. Sshh, sshh, sshh ...
EMILY. He'll have you killed if you try to do anything to him.
JERRY. We don't get killed around here, Emily, we just lose parts.
EMILY. No police, no police ...
LIN. All right, we won't, sshh, sshh, sshh, no police.

JERRY. Tell us what happened, Emily.

EMILY. He beat me up in the car and then we were going down the road to that little store — he was going to make me eat ice cream — and all of a sudden he got a real bad tummy ache; he can't eat spicy food; he needs to have his gall bladder out, but he's afraid to go to sleep for the operation, that someone won't let him wake up.

JERRY. How'd you get away?

EMILY. He had to run into the woods to have diarrhea. I took the car but I crashed.

JERRY. Why did he start hitting you?

EMILY. He'll be here, he'll come!

LIN. Sshh. Emily, why did he —

EMILY. *(To Jerry.)* He said you'd call in the morning and we'd make the movie because you didn't have the guts not to and I told him that before we start we hadda tell you I got a venereal disease. And he said: I gave it to *him,* I could give it to *you,* you were no better'n him; and I said maybe *he* gave it to *me* and he started bashing me and we went to get the ice cream ...

JERRY. I don't mean to make light of this, Emily, but after he beats the crap outta ya, does he usually go out for dessert?

EMILY. Whenever I eat ice cream, my throat swells all up and I can't breath.

STEPHEN. Jesus.

EMILY. Once, Calvin made me eat so much he hadda call 9-1-1! *I wish they'da let me die.*

JERRY. No, ya don't.

EMILY. You look so serious, you guys. God, that's nice.

JERRY. You're a major mess, Emily, ya know that?

EMILY. Yeah.

JERRY. Sort've a human industrial accident. *(She reaches out and clutches Jerry's hand. Outside, Cal rushes on, out of breath, his jacket in hand. During the following, he straightens himself, puts his jacket on ... and will head for the door.)*

EMILY. I never had a friend like you, Jerry.

JERRY. Yeah, well, as a friend, I'm telling you you're not

going back to him.

EMILY. Who's gonna take care of me? Where will I live?

JERRY. You can live with me. I'll take care of you.

EMILY. What would I have to do in exchange?

JERRY. We'll negotiate but not now. *(Stephen hands her two aspirin and holds a glass of water to her lips. Cal knocks at the door. A beat. Emily covers herself completely with the afghan, tries to disappear.)*

CAL. Steve? *(Another knock.)* Steve, it's me — the Reverend Calvin Rhodes.

JERRY. The Rev. Rhodes, stumper, can no longer be countenanced. Open the door.

CAL. Mrs. Ryder, are you there, dear?

STEPHEN. What're you gonna do?

JERRY. I'm just gonna have a few words with him about his behavior. Open the door. *(Jerry positions himself across the room. We may not notice him fishing in his saddlebag for something. Stephen opens the door.)*

CAL. I'm terribly sorry to bother you, Steve, but ... *(Cal steps in, takes in the scene, and peeks under the afghan where it's obvious Emily's hiding.)* Gee, I'm surprised to find you here, Emily. Jerry, nice to see you again. You see what you did to the car, Emily? I didn't take collision coverage on the vehicle. That's gonna be some pricey car rental. You hurt yourself? Good. Let this be a lesson. You use narcotics, then drive recklessly, you get hurt. Okay, Emmie, here we go.

JERRY. She's not going with you.

CAL. Sure she is. Up and at 'em, Emmie! *(Cal yanks Emily to her feet; she cries out. Stephen grabs Cal by the wrist.)*

STEPHEN. Don't do this, Cal. I think you should leave here for the night and go on back to the hotel. It'd be a lot better, ya understand what I'm sayin'? *(For a moment, Cal and Stephen are nose to nose, Cal's wrist locked in Stephen's hand.)*

CAL. You got a good grip there, Steve. *(Cal tries to break free coolly ... but Stephen's too strong.)*

STEPHEN. I'm givin' ya a heckuva good piece of advice. I want ya to take it.

CAL. Quit taking other people's advice a long time ago.

(Cal breaks free, turns ... to find Jerry with a snub nose .38 Police Super pointed at his crotch.)

STEPHEN. Aw, Jerry, what're ya doin' with that, man?

JERRY. Always carry it, stumper. Never know when you might want to make an exit.

CAL. I hope you have a permit for that, Jerry.

JERRY. Ninety grain, hollow point shells. Go in your urethra size of a bee-bee, come out your ass size of a cannonball.

STEPHEN. Jerry, are you nuts?

JERRY. Don't think so, but maybe, certainly possible. See if he's carrying anything.

STEPHEN. You gotta promise me first you're not gonna —

JERRY. I'm not promising you anything!

STEPHEN. Then, I'm sorry, I'm callin' the police. *(Stephen starts for the phone.)*

JERRY. You pick up that phone, Stephen, I swear to you I'll put a bullet in the back of your head, another in his, then one in mine. *(Stephen stops.)*

LIN. Lift your hands away from your body, please, Mr. Rhodes. *(Lin comes forward to take Cal's jacket off him and to pat him down.)*

CAL. Well, well, well, just like the old cowboy movies, huh, pardners? Enemies mere hours ago, they are bound together at the moment of crisis in pursuit of justice. I assure you I'm not armed. Proverbs Eighteen: "Death and life is in the power of the tongue." You don't use artillery against moral pygmies; one only requires the thumb of God's eternal damnation.

JERRY. That scares the unholy crap outta me, Cal, I can tell you that. *(Lin steps away from Cal — he's clean.)*

CAL. Thank you, Mrs. Ryder, I hope that was as gratifying for you as it was for me. All right, Jerry, you think you want to take me on, you and your oriental sister, hell, go ahead, turn me in to the authorities, fine. Miss Emily makes her accusations, they arrest me, we'll go to court, see what happens.

JERRY. We're not going to turn ya in, Cal.

CAL. Ah, little extortion, is it? Or do I simply walk out of your lives? You reform Miss Emily, she becomes a brain surgeon, you live happily ever after farming clean vegetables and fruit with your new bubba here. Am I getting warm with any of those scenarios, Jer?

JERRY. Uh-uh, you're cold.

STEPHEN. Jerry, wake up, wake up! What are we — vigilantes? Whudduya think, ya wanna go back to the wild west with people shootin' each other in the streets because they happen to disapprove of each other's behavior? Didn't you kill enough in Nam, man? Haven't we gotten past that? Think, Jerry, think: You understand what it means when you pull a gun on someone? What'd they teach us in Basic, Jerry? You pull a gun ...

JERRY. ... Someone's gotta die.

STEPHEN. And you're really prepared to deal with that here, tonight?

JERRY. Yeah. And you don't want to help me, fine, but I'm warnin' ya, stay out of my way. Now, you gonna gimme a hand here, brother?

STEPHEN. Help you kill a man — no, no, I'm not gonna help ya do that.

LIN. Jerry, listen to me a minute, don't say anything. When I left before, while I was walking, I started thinking about the photograph of South Vietnam's Chief of Police executing that Vietcong suspect on a street in Saigon in 1968. You remember that? The determination of guilt and the punishment were decided in an instant. And I imagined myself doing the same thing to Mr. Rhodes. But then I thought, what do I do with his mortal remains? Hear me out. I thought, first I would dissect him in pieces, looking for clues to his character, and then I would put the pieces into our septic tank in the fine mesh cages I haul my vegetables to and from the hydroponics lab in. I would add a booster of acid to the dissolvent Stephen put in the tank this afternoon.

STEPHEN. Lin.

LIN. Mr. Rhodes, you see, would seep out the leech lines and become a part of the landscape. In his death, he would be far more nutritive than in his life.

JERRY. What about the bones?
LIN. We pull the cages out in three weeks or so; the flesh will be gone. We break the bones down and put them in fifteen or twenty cement blocks. We build the first three or four courses of the cinder block fence around our house.
CAL. Well, well, well, I gotta admit that's good, that is a damn fine plan. Why I know people in New Jersey who would pay a great deal to avail themselves of your talents, Mrs. Ryder.
JERRY. Is this guy great?
LIN. Not even a little bit scared, are you, Mr. Rhodes?
CAL. I have a question for you, Jerry, just one, and that's what gives you the right to pass judgment on me? Am I worse than you?
JERRY. Shut up.
CAL. Make me! Do you crave less than I do?
JERRY. I said shut up.
CAL. And I said make me! Do you hate this gook whore any less than I do? Or this simple-minded parasite sucking out the marrow of your talent? Do you want to own and torment Emily any less than I do? What do you think you are, some kinda saint, some noble wounded martyr? No, as far as I can discern, you're just a loser strapped to a wheelchair the rest of your self-pitying life!
JERRY. Ouch, Cal. Ouchie. *(The gun remains fixed and pointed at Cal's crotch; but now the gun begins to shake.)*
STEPHEN. Jerry, the war's over, brother, let it go. Nobody has to die here tonight, brother. *(Slowly, Stephen has reached for and now takes the revolver from Jerry, then dumps it on the coffee table ... from where we may not see Lin pick it up.)*
CAL. You've got no guts, Jerry. You're all talk and slobber. You're a punk. A cripple.
STEPHEN. That's enough, Cal! Now, go on, get outta here — go!
CAL. Thank you, Steve, I believe I will. I believe I'll return to the hotel, take a bubble bath, devour that little mint patty they put on your pillow, and get some sleep. Come on, little bub. *(A beat.)* Simple decision, Emmie — stay or go? *(Torn,*

she looks to Jerry.)

JERRY. I can't take care of you.

EMILY. *(To Jerry.)* Don't be ... don't be mean to yourself.

STEPHEN. Don't leave with him, Emily.

EMILY. I have to.

CAL. Have to, Emmie?

EMILY. Want to.

STEPHEN. Stay here. We'll help you; we'll get help *for* you.

CAL. "Behold, how good and how pleasant it is for brethren to dwell together in unity!" Step aside, Steve. We can't all be me; some of us have to be the guys like you and Jerry. *(Cal shoves Stephen aside, grabs Emily again.)*

LIN. Take your hands off her, Mr. Rhodes. *(Cal yanks Emily toward the door, but Lin blocks the way.)*

CAL. Yes, may I help you?

LIN. She's somebody's daughter.

CAL. And?

LIN. She's somebody's little girl.

CAL. *And?*

LIN. She had a mother who loved her.

CAL. You grow tiresome, Mrs. Ryder. Emily's over the age of consent. The choice is hers.

LIN. Yes, all right. Then this is mine — my choice. *(He starts past her, but she puts the gun in his face.)*

STEPHEN. Lin, please, let's just let him go, let's just get him out of our life.

LIN. How?

EMILY. You got kids, Mrs. Ryder. You got your two little girls.

LIN. That's exactly why I should kill him. And Mr. Rhodes may have known Jerry wouldn't kill him, but he's not sure about me because, you see, Mr. Rhodes is afraid that I don't compute. What if I told you, Mr. Rhodes, I often dream of running away with a mysterious man I cannot resist, and for a moment when I first saw you I wondered if you were that man? What if I told you that after I saw Emily in her movie, I despaired somewhere deep inside of me that I would never have the opportunity to have sex with three adoring strangers. If I told you those things or things like those things, you might begin to think I do compute; but that would make you wrong. Because though surely you're right and there is a whore in every woman, there is also a mother who, oh yes, will compromise her girlhood dreams of love and marriage and will kill to protect her young so they might live a sweeter life than she.

CAL. Oh, Mrs. Ryder ... Lin ... despite your impassioned rhetoric, the truth, Lin, is that we bad men are more attractive than the supposedly decent, and you still want to run away with me. Emily noted when we first got here that this trailer smells like people just live here. To me, it smells like nothing so much as people decaying. You have only to go out the door with me to escape that smell.

LIN. Go away, Mr. Rhodes. Go far away. We understand each other. We know each other. I want to kill you — you understand that — but I don't want to live with it. But I will if you insist. So — simple decision: Stay, Mr. Rhodes, or go. Which?

CAL. Go.

LIN. Don't try to scare us or hurt us. *(Cal nods.)* A deal? *(Cal nods. Lin stares at him, into him ... and makes a decision we can't read yet.)* Seal it with me. With a kiss. *(She bends to him, puts her mouth to his. She kisses him and it's a moment before he responds, but he does ... and it's another moment before she has his tongue between her teeth, clamped there resolutely ... and bites into what's between her teeth, severing it from the rest. Cal screams. Blood runs from both their mouths. He gags and chokes. Mesmerized and immobilized, Stephen and Emily recoil and watch. Jerry's revulsion sends him out the door and down the ramp, where he sits in the night.)* You lied to me! I know you'd come back and hurt us! Look at me and listen very carefully! *(She thrusts the washcloth they used to clean Emily up into his mouth; she presses it to the remains of his tongue ... then holds her hand toward him, a piece of his tongue in her palm.)* I have this piece of your tongue. I can throw it away or I can put it in a bowl of ice and take it with us to the hospital. A tongue will not grow back but it can be reattached. Or I can take this washcloth away, put you out into the night, and let you bleed to death. Look me in my eyes and make me know this time that you won't come back. We were drunk, we kissed, we fell. *Look me in my eyes! (A beat ... and as the lights fade to half light, we hear Jerry start to chant outside.)*

JERRY. Left, left, left, right, left.
I don't know but I've been told
My best girl ain't stayin' home.
Ain't no use in phonin' back
Calvin's got her in the sack.

(Inside during the chant, Stephen wraps Cal in the afghan, helps him up, and out the door ... as Lin gets a small plastic bowl, fills it with ice cubes, and follows. The three of them go down the ramp and off, Lin and Stephen taking Cal to the hospital.)

Left, left, left right left.
If you crave to grunt and groan
Let your heart just turn to stone ...

Scene 8

Dawn. Jerry sits outside alone. Emily sleeps on the couch.

JERRY. *(Continuing.)*
Then you'll live your life alone
In a chair in an old stump's home.
(His voice fades under.)
Left, left, gimme your left, right, left ...
(Emily wakes with a start, panting, bolts upright.)

EMILY. Am I ... am I here? *(She finds herself alone. She calls.)* Mrs. Ryder? Mrs. Ryder...! *(Stephen, a towel around his neck, enters from the bedroom.)* Where's Mrs. Ryder? *(He points back toward the bedroom.)* Did you come back from the hospital? *Stephen nods.)* And he's ... is he ...

STEPHEN. He's fine. Or whatever he is. Reassembled.

EMILY. Where's Jerry? *(He points outside. A beat ... and Emily goes out. As she comes, Jerry begins to chant again.)*

JERRY. I don't know but I've been told
Ain't no use in phonin' home
Calvin's bought a Yidillac
And my baby's in the back.

EMILY. Can I be with you?

JERRY. Left, left, gimme your left, right, left ...

EMILY. Mr. Ryder says he ... that Calvin's okay ... *(Jerry doesn't respond. They remain in silence a moment.)* I got some medication problems, if ya know what I mean. I either need some medicine right about now or I'm gonna be in pretty bad shape here.

JERRY. Isn't it pretty clear, Emily, that I can't help you?

EMILY. We made a deal to take care of each other — that's not fair, Jerry. *(Jerry doesn't respond.)* Yesterday you said ... you said when Calvin asked you how come ya gave up and took your foot off that mine, you said, "I didn't give up, I don't give up" — what about that?

JERRY. Guy-talk. Big-man-talk.

EMILY. Yeah, well that really sucks! You're a quitter! That really disappoints me about you! *(A beat.)* Course who am I that people aren't allowed to disappoint me? *(The phone rings. Stephen doesn't move. The phone rings two, three times before he gets up and answers it ... as Lin, thinking he must be outside, comes in from the bedroom, wearing a robe, her hair wet and wrapped in a towel.)*

STEPHEN. *(Answering the phone.)* Hello.... Hello, little inky-stinky. How was the slumber party? Are you ready for school? Yes, honey, our friends have left. *(He turns his back. We can't hear what he's saying. Our focus goes back outside.)*

EMILY. Do you know where the word "companion" comes from, Jerry? Huh? It comes from the Latin word to share bread. He told me that. Once he brought this really gigantic French bread home from the store and we slathered it up with this fake, non-dairy butter and ate the whole thing while it was still warm, and it was gooshing butter all over our faces, and our hands were all greasy, and he would always remind me of that when he wanted to remind me we'd done stuff that was really nice and kinda romantic. But we both had diarrhea about eleven times from all that fake butter. So I guess it was only really romantic if ya didn't think about it past the good part. *(Jerry moves to Emily.)*

JERRY. You're a philosopher, Emily.

EMILY. Yeah, well that's always what I kinda thought I'd grow up to be. *(He holds his hand out to her. She takes it ... and then lays her head in his lap. He strokes her gently as our focus goes back inside.)*

STEPHEN. Honey, honey, I can't help it, now don't be mad at me, we'll do it another time. Look, I gotta go, honey, I love you, bye. *(Stephen hangs up the phone.)*

LIN. They all right?

STEPHEN. The usual: Linny's upset because Mackie and Beverly wouldn't let her listen to them talk about boys all night. She had to watch "Donna Reed" re-runs. She wants me to take her to breakfast before school but not Mackie or Beverly.

LIN. You should do it.

STEPHEN. How d'ya take a kid to breakfast from where we are, Lin?

LIN. Are we going to stop speaking to them? Are we going to let the parents of their friends raise them? Call her back, tell her you'll come get her. *(A beat.)*

STEPHEN. What's the number? *(Lin moves close to Stephen, takes the phone and begins to dial the number on their rotary dial telephone. When she's several numbers into it ...)* You got toothpaste on your mouth.

LIN. I brushed my teeth a lot. *(A beat as she stops dialing and they stare at each other.)* Wipe it off. *(He puts the phone down ... wets his finger from his mouth and gently wipes the toothpaste away from her mouth. Her hand presses his against her face ... and then she brings his head to her shoulder, holds him there, almost as if he were her child ... as the stage goes black.)*

PROPERTY LIST

Folder with papers (STEPHEN)
Pen (STEPHEN)
Cutting board (JERRY)
Knife (JERRY)
Zucchini (JERRY)
Tray with cheese and crackers (LIN)
Carrots (julienne sliced) (LIN)
Bag (EMILY) with:
    needlepoint cloth
    needles
    thread
Manila envelope (CAL)
Wrist watch (CAL)
Plastic medication bottle with capsules (CAL)
Wine bottle (STEPHEN)
Wine glass
Ramp for wheelchair (STEPHEN)
Purse (EMILY) with:
    small vial of 'cocaine'
Cigar case (STEPHEN)
1 sneaker (LIN)
Children's toys (LIN)
Stuffed animals (LIN)
Pot of sauce on stove (CAL)
Lightweight zipper jacket with Dallas Cowboys logo on it (LIN)
Storage box (STEPHEN) with:
    tackle box
    2 fishing rods
2 jugs of dissolvent (CAL)
Eye glasses (EMILY)
Manuscript (EMILY)
Book (LIN)
Notebook (LIN)

Highlighter pen (LIN)
Cigar (CAL)
Glass with herbs in water (CAL)
Dictionary (CAL)
Plates (STEPHEN)
Drinking glasses (STEPHEN)
Chopsticks (STEPHEN)
Fork (STEPHEN)
Saucepan (LIN)
Flashlight (LIN)
Batteries for flashlight (LIN)
Afghan (STEPHEN)
Washcloth (JERRY)
Aspirin (STEPHEN)
Glass of water (STEPHEN)
Saddlebag (JERRY)
.38 police super pistol (JERRY)
Small plastic bowl (LIN)
Ice cubes (LIN)
Towels (STEPHEN, LIN)

SOUND EFFECTS

Phone rings
Car horn
Van horn

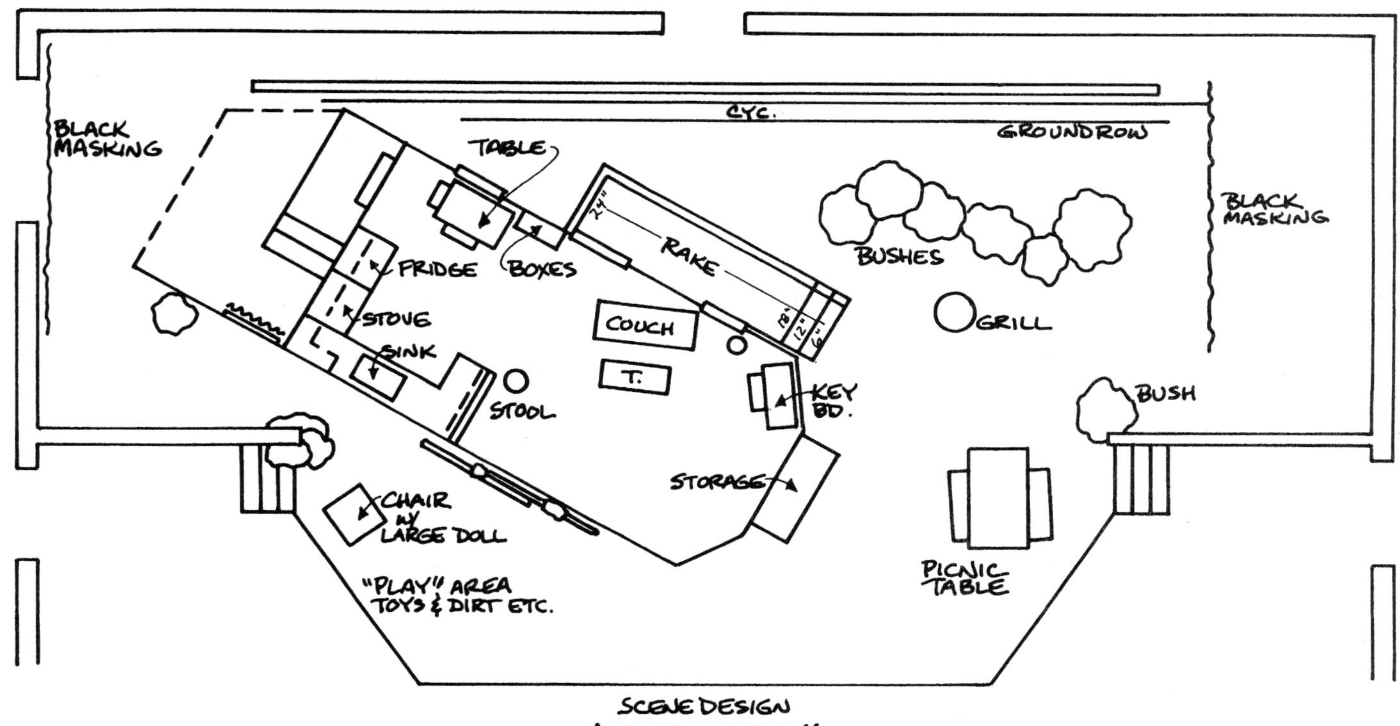

SCENE DESIGN

"STUMPS"

(DESIGNED BY JIM BILLINGS FOR NEW MEXICO REPERTORY THEATRE)

NEW PLAYS

DR

440 P